THE PITFALLS OF HOW, WHEN, WHERE AND WHY TO HIRE LAWYERS AND HOW TO USE A CONSULTANT TO DO SO AND LOWER YOUR LEGAL FEES

By: Stephen Schnitzer, Esq.

iUniverse, Inc.
New York   Bloomington

The Pitfalls of How, When, Where and Why To Hire Lawyers And How to Use A Consultant To Do So And Lower Your Legal Fees

iUniverse books may be ordered through booksellers or by contacting:

iUniverse
1663 Liberty Drive
Bloomington, IN 47403
www.iuniverse.com
1-800-Authors (1-800-288-4677)

Because of the dynamic nature of the Internet, any Web addresses or links contained in this book may have changed since publication and may no longer be valid. The views expressed in this work are solely those of the author and do not necessarily reflect the views of the publisher, and the publisher hereby disclaims any responsibility for them.

ISBN: 978-1-4502-3988-2 (sc)
ISBN: 978-1-4502-3989-9 (ebk)

Printed in the United States of America

iUniverse rev. date: 09/29/2010

Table of Contents

Dedication

This book is dedicated to all of the people who accepted the need to obtain it, read it and follow its advice as best that thought they should or understand to how do so.

Preface

Lawyering is a Profession!

Lawyering is a profession, however, so is prostitution! We may say that both are valuable to society although some might differ preferring one over the other. Rumor has it that the Garden of Eden Snake was the first lawyer. He advised Adam and Eve as to God's Laws and how to avoid them. God alone had told them what to do or not before the apple incident and their banishment. The rest is history and lawyers were set free as the Snake wandered off too into society ad the legal profession evolved. This brings us to current day history and how to behave if you find the need to throw yourself into today's snake pit of the legal profession.

As usually occurs within the Universe, there are parallel understandings from which help and interpretation can be gathered. Until probably only the last decade or two the medical profession has blinded society into virtually absolute submission to their medical directions whether competent, accurate or even beneficial. The pouring over effect to the legal community (lawyers and doctors being pretty much regarded in the same manner of reverence by the public -i.e.: necessary professionals) is that the public has been subtly led into blind acceptance and also of the advice of lawyers without question as they have with doctors. This is a phenomenon to be recognized and to avoid.

Finally, you must appreciate that lawyers like doctors are licensed for the full range of medical or legal undertakings. That means they have the right to project a legal ability to do so. Accordingly, a physician's license is as a "doctor and surgeon." However, in the area of medical board specialty and limited hospital privileges it is today very unlikely that a tissue community medical director would allow an ear doctor to book you in for heart surgery or pulmonary treatment. Moreover, given the extent of his hospital privileges, an ear doctor would not even try. Not so with lawyers. If they think your matter has sufficient economic value they are likely to take it on convincing you of their own diligence even in a specialty area either partially or wholly unknown to them. The object is for you to engage their services and they will learn on the job even if they have to call up friends who practice in the unknown to them area and pick their brain or engage their services too.

In conclusion since the snake left Eden, the area of legal malpractice in the last few years is one the biggest emerging concerns to the profession. The ever-growing body of professional legal malpractice actions directly reflects today's problems of choosing a lawyer competent, willing and actually able to represent you. For this reason this book effort has been undertaken to provide you with the best ideas of how to go about selecting or replacing your attorney. Ergo: A simple verse: Eenie-Meenie-Minie-Moe, Esq. what you really need to know in getting or replacing your lawyer?

The verse sets the tenor of what you should read slowly and carefully and absorb as best as possible. When you put this book aside you need to think about what it is saying to you and what it requires you to do for your own benefit. It is not a blueprint but rather a tool to help guide you.

"Kill All the Lawyers"
Shakespeare and everyone else who ever thought about it.

Introduction

More than any other country, America has become a society of lawyers. Their influence is disproportionate to the number of lawyers in the population which is not unusual if you consider both the nature of our legal system (adversarial) and the growth of our legal culture historically. Many of the tinkerers of the Constitution and since have been lawyers. A startling number of presidents have been lawyers. This is similarly true of the legislators in both state and federal governments and key department heads in the institutions which regulate, shape and control government function.

Finally, it is assiduously true in business. Virtually all large companies have internal general counsel legal staff who themselves rely upon a host of outside specialty counsel. Their purpose is to make certain the businessmen who control the business enterprise fall within the legal and regulatory schemes guiding their particular business and do not otherwise err. More particularly in earlier days before recrimination of in-house counsel their preponderant goal was to aid and protect the inner business circle from harm simply because management may have made an error. Said differently, the lawyers cover the back door of business, although frequently the predominant owners or their children enjoy the benefits of legal education.

In most states there are statutes which deal with errant professionals and businesses. They are often designated to be consumer fraud statutes. Certainly, New Jersey has one, and it has been well developed over the years. However, at the outset when lawyers first sued lawyers upon such legal theories (a rare commodity) and focused their attention on their legal brethren, judges (who are former lawyers) divined their legal interpretation that the consumer fraud statutes and their triple damage penalties and possible awards of legal fees do not reach lawyers. Accordingly, lawyers insulate themselves to create a protective moat around presumptive errant activities. Thus, it is not difficult to reach an appropriate overall conclusion that lawyers are in the primary position of effecting the very laws which might be considered dramatic to others but which are nullified to insulate lawyers. This is the ballpark in which you are playing. This is why you need a guide to bring you through the wilderness of the legal system (no matter what you might think your own understanding of it is) just as did Lewis & Clark to get into the new territories. Certainly to convince oneself by your own confidence that your ability is so well developed that you are likely to alone ferret it and will stumble on to the right pathway by accuracy of your own design (harsh as it may seem) is foolhardy. The uninitiated are by a lack of necessary background unlikely to know how to move within the legal system about which one is clearly uneducated, untrained, and doesn't have the foggiest idea of what it is really all about. Ergo: The reason for this book.

Accordingly, it is necessary to understand from the outset that in large effect lawyers historically and currently control our society which in large measure is not surprising given the public's disproportionate lack of understanding of how it works; how to modify it; and where to lobby for and gain influence. This is not information generally enjoyed by the lay members of the public. Ergo again: The reason for this book.

It should also be constantly bore in mind that unlike any other groups, lawyers are able to enforce within the society a hierarchy structure which protects them within the inner-circle far better than those less likely situated in our society. The first reason is legal education itself. Having created the system; studied the system; and worked within the system; the newly emerging young lawyer over the years develops an understanding of how to work around the fringes of the system particularly when it comes to preferring the lawyer's rights over those of clients. Therefore, it can hardly be said that in engagements of a lawyer that you are dealing on a level playing field because you do not know what the lawyer does know about the workings of the legal system, and you are otherwise calculated to become blinded by the light of their legal magic or words and ideas which are new, foreign and alien. It is difficult to understand your own case if you do not understand how the game plays out in court or before and what are the circumstances of what you must prove or disprove and at what levels (burdens of proof).

Indeed, a well known lawyer who sat at the top of a very large firm (and collected a much greater salary under his capacity as Lord Master) had the simple chore of telling disgruntled clients who had lost their cases what they had never heard at the outset, namely that fifty percent of all cases are lost which certainly was pithy advice that seems a little too late at the end especially if the loss could have been prevented at the beginning.

Most commonly, if the general patriarchs (senior firm counsel) do not give the advice needed to handle your case but rather turn it over to much younger members. These lawyers are not so initiated in the law, seeking instead a distinction of being able to claim a position as a member of a lofty, important firm but to receive by comparison a salary which was short-shriffed and a caseload that would make him overworked by any definition. The result is underpaying staff and lawyers in such firms while overloading them with work at the same time the senior members of the firm consider themselves social butterflies and rainmakers (business getters). This is not a smooth running operation overall to which one would wish to bring their important matter so that it could receive proper attention and diligence. That is not to say a good result cannot happen in such a structure, but the outcome that is most predictable depends upon the dedication and guise of the entrusted lawyer about which there can be no outcome certainty, even if things look good at the beginning. This can always change especially since in the lower ranks of the underappreciated attorneys there is a greater tendency to break away from the firm to either go out on your own (if your skills are sufficient) or to see a better position or join an in-house staff or government. What unfortunately occurs is that under these circumstances, your actual lawyer with whom you should have bonded disappears some time during the game and you are left either to try to bond with someone new and to what may be their different impression of how to handle the matter away from the discussion and original understandings of game plans made with your first lawyer. Moreover, you may not feel comfortable with the replacement team.

Lawyers are hardly a world of their own. They are supported by a large group of secretaries, paralegals, supervisors, junior partners, senior partners, office managers and the list does not end there. In a big firm that is a lot of people to interface with and to be polite to throughout the day. In fact, it is one of the reasons why many lawyers who start out in a bigger firms often seek the comfort, privacy and personal settings in much smaller settings including smaller general counsel offices and/or private practices on their own or with just a few other lawyers. These independent souls require less of the nurturing by others and are more likely to be self-starting, independent, and self-possessed in terms of an overall belief in the ability, energy, and quality of their skills. That does not always mean that lesser is more, but it is one thing to keep in mind. However, these small-group lawyers are no less accurately aware of the need and ability to protect themselves than are members of the big firm entourages. Simply because a lawyer is in a smaller firm does not mean he is any better self-guided towards clients than if he or she were in a larger structure.

Chapter One

Re-Introduction

Read the introduction! It sets the tenor for what you are about to read and learn. Many readers think it is unimportant, and often they are right. However, not this time for such a conclusion. The introduction gives you the flavor of what you need to think about and keep in the back of your mind as you assess what you are reading and how it can, should or will apply to you in your matter.

There is no particular order to this book. It is topical. It is giving you the headings of what you need to do or what it is perceived that you should know. However, by using the chapter index, you will be able to familiarize and re-familiarize yourself more quickly on the key line-items as they develop at different stages of need.

The book is not here to urge you to any conclusion of engagement except that you do so with your eyes open knowing realistically what to expect and not expect. Further, it is designed to help you get through what can become an unforgettable series of legal proceedings and help you become self-taught in what to expect.

Chapter Two

In the Lawyer's Defense

For the conscientious practitioner, lawyering is no casual matter. It takes a substantial amount of thought, dedication, sacrifice to the scheduling of more formal matters or family affairs because of the need to suddenly address an emergent problem or a client's needs. Very often this may happen several times throughout the day. This makes the lawyer seem distant or unreachable if the clients cannot readily contact them and enjoy what they feel is sufficient time to address their matters and personal concerns. It gives the appearance of being ignored. The same is true when you reach the lawyer and he is hurried or otherwise indicates that he does not have time in this moment for you. These are expectable conditions but they do not betoken well for the attorney/client relationship unless the client understands and truly appreciates these difficult circumstances. However, the pitfalls can also be that the lawyer for some particular reason is either ignoring the client or the client's matter and really is not sufficiently otherwise engaged. This leads sometimes to conditions of dysfunction on the lawyer's part because they are the ones that have accepted a professional engagement to "do the right thing." There is a subtle understanding among lawyers that there is always a file (naturally of some client) which you hate and cannot pick up or touch or go near until the very last minute. On the other hand, many lawyers are "Eleventh Hour Charlies" and cannot get about it until they are forced to by court time limits or other procedural matters which specify when they have to act or lose the chance to do so. This is not a lawyer that you want because by doing everything literally at the last minute there is a high likelihood that the ball is dropped and the game is over before the anticipated trial or other best legal shot can be taken for you. Dropped time periods is the most common episode for the suing of lawyers whether it is a Statute of Limitations or failure to respond to papers. In the older days, judges used to be much more lenient in allowing reopening, but now with the court calendar so crowded and less forgiving judges embenched, the easier way to be is that the court will stick to the time limits which bar your moving forward, and if there is any difficulty that you should consider if to sue your lawyer.

Another primary example of the development inherently of grievances against lawyers arises in the settlement of cases themselves. Settlements are good things. They bring mellowness to the proceedings and end the financial bloodletting of lawyers by reaching a compromise that might restore human relationships between the parties. They are not, however accomplished, without some cost particularly in terms of insulation of the attorneys. The recent development of the case law in <u>New Jersey</u> provides that despite how the matter was handled (properly vs. improperly in the workup or during the proceedings) if the client settles the matter at any time including before, during, or after trial this settlement event basically eliminates virtually any and all basis to sue the lawyer (absent some very virulent concept that in inspiring the settlement the lawyer defrauded the client). To prevent this type of allegation, most settlements are placed on the record in any substantial matter and the client specifically examined about their understanding of the settlement; compulsion in reaching it; satisfaction with their own attorney to which a negative indication ends the proceeding and aborts the settlement. Obviously, if you think your lawyer is not well advising you, then you are not being well guided into settling and it will not be approved. Therefore, not only has the client settled the case under the disability of a lack of reservation to sue the lawyer but he has also testified under oath of perjury that he finds the lawyer well reasoned and acceptable in their relationship. Again the lawyer lands on his feet in terms of attorney-client relationship no matter what went on before.

Against this backdrop it is most important to understand that there are unperceived issues of a fundamental psychological nature which can impair even the best of attorney-client relationships. When a client goes to a lawyer they are admitting the need for someone to help think best with them and for them! This is not something that is not natural. As people in the evolution process, we were taught to nurture our own style and beliefs to see us through on our own two feet as to what we need. This is a deeply engrained instinct which has subordinate considerations since our nuclear family (our spouses, children, and business associates subordinate to us) have come to rely upon us as the leaders within the family unit. Now all of a sudden the family leader genius has to sort out legal difficulties by getting someone else conspicuously to think for him at substantial expense. This has a potential to cause even a well-adjusted person substantial angst and turmoil in terms of developing a conflict with their own accepted attorney-client relationships. Unfortunately, often the client's response is one either rejects the lawyer's advice out of hand without thinking, resents it, resents the need to have it, acts against it, ignores it totally, or seeks to jibe or otherwise present resentment to the lawyer himself. Most often one can see this in divorce matters where anger afflicted by the failure of the marital relationship is so overwhelming that being unable to reach a spouse or former spouse the client misperceives a right to vent on the lawyer or to misaddress anger toward him. This is a mistake; it impairs completely the entire working relationship but it is not uncommon and it is very difficult to prevent against. This is why the selection of a lawyer with whom you can work is most important. This decision involves finding a lawyer who will tell you what you need to know whether you want to know it or not because that is his job. Accordingly, he is truthfully less concerned about being let go and having an inability to garner legal fees than he is in deliberately discharging his obligations to you of full and apt disclosure. This undertaking involves telling the client when they are off base rather than sitting in the back like a choirboy and simply muttering "Amen." It is particularly unclever for a client to find a lawyer with whom he can work positively; pay to have the matter taken and then abuse the relationship in such a way that the lawyer can and will be relieved as counsel as a result of which the original legal undertaking is jeopardized, and a lawyer once well found at the outset is lost to your cause for absolutely no good reason. It is a result of the client being selfish for which there is no actual need.

Chapter Three

Civil, Criminal and In-Between Matters

Criminal matters are the most unpleasant and often require good legal talent. Therefore, selecting an attorney who professes to do criminal law without either any real background as a prosecutor or public defender while he claims to do such specialized work (and handles all sorts of other general legal affairs) may not be the specific level that one requires to maintain their liberty. If you are taken to protecting yourself by being represented by someone who dabbles in the criminal law it is not the best of advice to succumb. It is, however, not unusual for a criminal lawyer also to be conspicuously involved in matrimonial affairs since the level of argument is particularly virulent in both practice streams and the talents required for successful outcome are not terrible far different.

Criminal proceedings are brought by governments and one is usually forewarned as to when they are coming. Preparation for legal problems will be discussed in another Chapter.

Civil matters and disputes can either be brought by governments for fines and penalties or to abort improper behavior or by anyone else in the community for general money relief lawsuits, tortious behavior, business disputes and the like. These are not criminal events, although in the course of such proceedings it may turn in that direction. Ny way of example, think of the children of a ward who seeks civilly to replace the trustee by alleging a theft of their parents' assets for which criminal prosecution then develops. If you suspect this can happen, then you need also at the outset to also consult a criminal lawyer to determine what rights (5th Amendment bar against self-incrimination) you might have at hand in the civil matter. In the selection process of your civil attorney, you need someone able and experienced to work in conjunction with criminal counsel. However, such civil attorneys may come forward with their own suggestion and out of politeness for good politic it is often necessary at least to meet with their designee criminal attorney.

In the big firm you will likely be referred to their own criminal division. This should be avoided. It puts too much control in one firm and a smaller lawyer in the criminal division may be born to the will of an older civil attorney in the firm. There are issues behind the scenes you may never know or sort out but it disallows the freedom of action and apt defense advice you may well need later on but not receive. It is better to pick your own "A team" than have a new lawyer who is an ostensible stranger to you do so. [1]

---

1   See Chapter as to referrals which will further guide you.

Chapter Four

Private Do-Gooder Actions

There are many public organizations such as the Southern Society for Legal Affairs, the A.C.L.U., ethnic law groups, and any variety of private entities (e.g. American Indian Legal Affairs) that bring actions at their election which favor private citizens and aid the public good. Your ability to pick a lawyer in these circumstances is virtually non-existent but you may assure yourself that you have a whole team ready, willing and able to support your claim should they elect to take your case. These do-gooder lawyers do not take action until there is reasonable belief as to a positive outcome and most likely when undertaken are successful. A good example is that several years ago a young black man was beaten up by three intoxicated Ku Klux Klan members who were recruiting new members at a State Fair because they perceived his social involvement with a white woman. The Grand Wizard of the Ku Klux Klan was sued by the Southern Law Conference although he never met the other defendant individuals, and he was not at the Fair. A verdict in excess of $1 million was awarded against the Ku Klux Klan's Grand Wizard. Obviously the case had nothing to do with the 16- or 17-year old battered plaintiff but he was certainly well represented and his injuries addressed by use of virulently superior lawyers. It is in this manner that the law evolves by bringing new ideas and new principles to the process of decision which helps to guide social behavior and cautions people as to what to do and not do in their behavior. Yet again, this displays the significant sociological influence of lawyers.

There are also many public and statutory remedies of benefit available to citizens for which they need lawyers. Probably foremost among these is our Workmen's Compensation Statutes which protect the workers and employees against crippling injuries and everlasting poverty. Another example is a social security system and its benefits. Generally lawyers who work within these system structures and appear in specialty legal arenas do not receive fees from the clients but rather from the system. However, this does not mean one can afford a lack of attention in engaging such counsel since the results of various lawyers appear far different. In these systems some lawyers prepare their matters substantially and diligently while others prefer that they have instead of hundreds of such matters, rather thousands of these cases are settled on a lower-end because there is not going to be much more benefit to the lawyer (and what is the difficulty as to the client). Very often matters in these offices are handled almost exclusively by paralegals and low-salary employees who do not know or understand the matters and are simply processing papers to which there is little or no thought to either the work relationship or lack of training. Ultimately on the day in question a lawyer picks up 8 or 10 files and reviews them to figure out his best tactic on the client to convince them to settle the matter so it is brought to a prompt and quick conclusion without any further energy or expense to his office. This does not tend to maximize the result, and early settlements of these matters, unless they are for the full amounts of the awards due, are not the best idea.

Chapter Five

Mediation and Arbitration

These are specialty proceedings conducted during the course of civil litigation. While they may appear to the uninitiated not to be particularly inherently important (since the ultimate goal is the trial itself hopefully with a well-meaning jury) this is not the case. There appears to be little need among some practitioners to seriously address such interim proceedings with high energy. This is a mistake and it is likely that many larger law firms have lawyers who are particularly geared to success at these interim presentations. The reason they are important is because the judicial system is very backed up. This is nothing new. It has been going on for years. Judges want their cases settled. If one-tenth of people with a case tried their cases, there would be no system. Justice would break down because the resources are not great enough to fully try even a very small caseload. Accordingly, when a case has been mediated or arbitrated and you are now down to interfacing with a judge at a trial setting, one of the first things they want to know is what was the arbitration or medication outcome because they use that as a template for settlement discussions and their own perceptions. Said differently, why shouldn't they? I particularly remember a mediation session where the defendant had a lawyer who freely admitted he knew little or nothing about the file and the mediator (who was a lawyer) made a determination of value of $5 million which is revealed in the court's file for the court to note. It was very difficult for the defense to shy away from that mediation proceeding award, and even though there was a high likelihood that the case was time-barred, they ended by settling the case for multiples of six figures.

Finally, the nature of the proceeding needs to be understood. Americans enjoy an adversarial system. It means that the lawyer's job is to muster up the evidence best suited to state your position and to overcome the opposing position. The judge is to follow Bill O'Reilly's mantra of "fair and impartial." Does this always occur? "No." Does something occur? "Yes." Are there proceedings that can be regarded with surprise by an unfair undercurrent in the regard? "Yes, most certainly."

Are you likely ever to prove that something wrong went on? "No." What then is the solution? The simple answer is to pick a lawyer with whom you are well bonded who will see the matter through and enjoy a well adjusted relationship with him in terms of gathering up the evidence for presentation of why your legal position which should be leading either to an effective settlement or successful trial outcome. Something less than that does not even put you in the game.

However, you should not be confused that although the system is adversarial, that does not betoken aspects of disrespect between counsel which is strictly forbidden. This is the proper level of behavior between the lawyer and opposition counsel which is not a vendetta but rather the playing out of the established Rules of Practice in a civilized manner in an established System of Justice.

Is the system perfect? "No," but it is a lot better than what occurs in many other "civilized and uncivilized jurisdictions." In many civilized places of the world when accused, you are jailed immediately, and you find your own way out. There is no presumption of innocence. In less civilized places, the lawyers who are regarded as intellectuals are simply jailed or murdered when the revolution comes. That is certainly no benefit to society and leads to the collapse of an established justice system or predictably the citizens without greater wealth or influence become nothing more than peeons. As controversial as lawyers may seem to you, they still remain the last bastion of due process and human rights.

Chapter Six

Pre-Hiring Considerations

Some people pride themselves on never having missed a day or two of school. I suspect that the percentage of those people is much lower than the people who could pride themselves on never being involved in the American Justice System. Someday almost everyone is going to find themselves in a situation where they are going to need a lawyer for whatever reason (real estate, divorce, estate planning, civil lawsuits, traffic violations, workmen's compensation) and the category can become seemingly endless).

"To be forewarned is to be forearmed"

<u>The Sizzle of Trouble</u>

The common experience recently is to "forget the sizzle" and "where is the beef?" However, before you get to it when you know you are going to sue or be sued or have issues in court the sizzle is already apparent, and there is a need to prepare the beef for cooking.

Gathering of Evidence

Evidence of every type or nature (e.g. direct and indirect) is what controls the outcome of legal matters. A plaintiff has a burden of proof which depending upon the type of matter will vary as to criminal prosecution ("beyond a reasonable doubt") or civil actions. In either case type, you have to establish proofs by competent evidence. In a criminal matter, you need say nothing, but when a *prima facie* case (one sufficiently established to prevail at first blush) is put in by the State you need to overcome it or suffer the likelihood of a conviction. Similarly, if you put in a *prima facie* case in a civil case which can be overcome by competent evidence that contests your proofs. Evidence, its mustering up by discovery or proofs available at the outset, and its use are what lawsuit cases are all about.

The handling of evidence including how to place it in the proceeding before the judge or jury is the lawyer's job. That is an art, and very often competent evidence can get and does get excluded because the lawyer is not prepared to work with it in a knowing way or is not up on the Rules of Evidence. Ergo: A good case suffers defeat principally from a lack of skill of the legal magician (your lawyer). In many cases there is no need to be particularly concerned with your own gathering up of evidence. This is true in most injury cases where the lawyer should be skilled in getting the required information such as hospital records, medical reports, and the like. He will also need to get you examined by experts including physicians willing to testify to your loss, injuries and harm. However, many lawyers may not fully and competently obtain and retrieve evidence or potential causes of action that you may have arising some other problems other than an apparent car accident which might including road design or traffic developments leading to liability from municipalities or others and enhancement of the financial aspects of your matter. This is one of the major reasons lawyers in the negligence field are sued.

Obviously there are several types of evidence to be gathered by the lawyer. In the situation above some of it is preexisting hospital records and other newly formed evidence of which are created to style your case such as expert's reports from people you never met before the injury.

However, in nontraditional accident settings when you detect a "sizzle," the time has come pre-suit to gather up your evidence and to begin to create a safe harbor for your affirmative claims or defenses.[2]

When your intuition tells that there is going to be a legal dance, you should and must begin to consider getting legal advice both as to the gathering up of evidence; what should be the nature of the evidence itself and the circumstances (legal and otherwise) of how to gather the evidence so it is competent and not tainted, and therefore, useable. It is one thing to do know what went on, but it is another thing to know early on whether you have a trustworthy admissible document or verbal statement that can be admitted into evidence at trial.

For example, suppose you believe that you have been the subject of job discrimination in the employee relationship or sexual harassment. In the first instance you have been negatively referred to on some basis concerning sex, sexual orientation, race, religion, culture, or some other defined category. In another instance you might feel that you have been sexually exploited and are now being held out to ridicule, further exploitation, or have been fired because somebody's wife or partner wanted you to be. Very often after the discharged event the client seeks now

---

2 "He who hesitates is lost." "A stitch in time saves nine." "You snooze, you lose."

only to engage counsel to try and redress any exploitation that they suffered. However and unfortunately, the "evidence" that is most likely to exist after the event date is usually comments of the "he said, she said" nature which are of no particular real value since the aggrieved client has no real underlying evidence. Accordingly, being aware of the sizzle situation, those clients that engaged counsel weeks or months before the final discrimination events occurred employing an effective system of gathering evidence to preserve the claim should lead to a positive outcome. Some people think that they will be able to rely upon what their coworkers heard or their own perception of what is offensive. However, subjective standards of what offends one person is not necessarily sufficient evidence where the judicial system relies upon objective standards or whether a reasonable person would have been offended. It would shock you to find out what low things have been and can be said with impunity in the employee relationship. Therefore, obtaining counsel and receiving good preparation advice from an experienced lawyer in employee relationships (and not someone who dabbles in everything) should be a well-established pre-suit undertaking.

Some people who are about to become such clients set off gathering "evidence" themselves. Often they will seek to gather "evidence" by taking or removing documents which might be forbidden under employment confidentiality agreements, including the employee manual. Under some circumstances, it might be considered theft. This is why you need a lawyer to read any documents or manuals to make certain that you are not over the line of scrimmage before the ball is hiked thereby leading to the "exclusion of evidence" and a revealed improper evidence gathering which could lead to successful claims against you either civil or possibly criminal.

Some people think to gather "evidence" by using tape recording devices, telephone recording devices, or other sophisticated electronic equipment such as self-starting monitoring devices which is triggered by a telephone call. However interesting may be the "evidence" gathered in many instances, its gathering might be illegal and may lead to great difficulties. Evidence exclusions are associated with clients who clearly violated applicable law in gathering such "evidence."

In most states there exist sophisticated wiretaping laws that vary from state to state. As a general rule, some states prohibit the tape recording of a conversation that is not announced in advance or such calls which are taped from body or briefcase devices and exclude the "evidence" gathered. Virtually all forbid surveillance recording devices secreted within the home or business, because the "evidence" gathered is not by a a participant to the conversation. For this reason and this reason alone it is essential for an experienced lawyer guide you in the gathering of "evidence" during the sizzle period following which the failure to do so, and therefore, your empty hands are exposed. Only an experienced lawyer from state to state can tell you what the standards are in their particular community.

Chapter Seven

Areas of Concern
"The Titanic Ballroom Reception"

In going through the door of a law firm once you have seen the need or heard the sizzle, you will note that some of them are designed with facades and accoutrements which make the ballroom of the Titanic look like a New York courthouse's public bathroom. All that space and flash costs money and it is designed to impress. There is no accident afoot. The one who pays for it are clients of the firm.

You will also commonly see very often row after row of various size conference rooms (usually not filled) and often with names written after some category important to the managing partners whether it is hotels or former governors or presidents. You are also likely to see in these places pictures of the senior managers of the firm with their arms perched around politicians presuming there was some deep relationship existing between these important people which is most unlikely. You have to remember that it is there for advertising and your perception (sic: misperception) that these lawyers are people of influence and may call upon their "big friends" to help your matter which is a fully ridiculous notion. Lawyers of confidence as to their skills need not so prostitute themselves although an occasional picture within the law office itself from a public person is certainly not errant. However, when overdone, the obvious goal is to sell you a bill of goods for the purposes of opening your wallet.

Actually in these large firms initial and ongoing consultations with the lawyer occurs in such conference rooms which is booked in advance for meeting. This has several advantages for the law firm itself some of which are not obvious and developed only when you think about them over the years. These rooms are stated to have a schedules so if you get there at 9:00 A.M. and the conference room is booked until your scheduled meeting at 10:00 A.M., you cannot start your meeting. By the time they change the coffee and donuts, late arrivals of any other participants or firm members, and polite salutations you can soon dwindle to a much smaller period of effective time beyond your control. This would not be true in a smaller law office where you are allowed or invited to go into the lawyer's own office lair. That is where you will see what betokens his personalty and be able to make your own assessment.

Many lawyers' personal offices are outfitted with pictures and relics gathered up over the years which gives you a human opinion of them and allows you to be much better guided in whether you are comfortable or not with his person.

Let's say the lawyer's office is completely barren with no files, children's pictures on the walls, photographs of the family and dog or anything else in the background. You might conclude that this is cold and sterile and belong to a person who is not whom you feel you would be able to develop a working relationship. On the other hand, you might see an office filled with other things with which you could associate leading to a positive reaction. You are kept out of this in a firm area where conferences are held only at the designated rooms. Usually, the truth of the matter in such firms is that the lawyers are working in small cubicle offices hardly bigger than a jail cell from which they are forced to work and you are properly excluded from these garrets (unless of course you are a firm "rainmaker" big boss). It is no accident. You are lead to believe everything is done on a grand and luxurious scale by the office flash while the people who are to serve your legal needs are themselves the subject of short-shrift and are shouldering their workloads most probably into the firm's firebox as quickly as their caseload will allow. Quite frankly, it is not the fault of these young lawyers; it is how the system has built up and how a few legal patriarchs are able to sit on top of their own firms where the very buildings being used are likely owned by them and a majority of the money generated are received by them "until death do they part." You have to bear in mind that lawyers rarely retire except for health reasons or death and many of them are active into their mid-80's with sufficient acumen to know what they are doing or how to stay on the firm's payroll by getting money for themselves from those in the lower structure of the firm.

Banishment from the lawyer's inner office also prohibits an exposure usually to the lawyer's secretary or support staff, paralegals and the like. These days most lawyers are not totally alone wherein they work up the case; type the court papers; photocopy them; and present them. He or she, even in a mid-sized firm, is often one of a team of may (i.e.: lawyers and secretaries or lawyers, paralegals or secretaries/paralegals). Obviously, the support staff can be as important as the lawyer, but if you determine any weakness in terms of personnel support then you need look no further and leave.

It is also extremely important to see the back room operations to determine how effectively the staff works with each other. Some lawyers get a new secretary or paralegal every few months and if so this tends to create a great strain on the contents of his materials which they are required to pick up and move forward. Thus, in dealing with your lawyer (particularly over what may become several years) there needs to develop a familiar relationship including with the staff so ideas and information can be effectively communicated back and forth. In viewing these circumstances you may determine that the support team does not think much of their own lawyer(s). If that is their opinion, why should yours be any different?

Accordingly, there is much to be gathered from your need to view these relationship levels and there is certainly nothing wrong with asking that the support staff be introduced to you and attend your meetings and work with you. That is especially true if the lawyer is relying upon the paralegals to accomplish the results for which they may be uninformed (or misinformed) having gotten only general exchanges from your work sessions. However, they do not know what is important to you except from secondhand information. Naturally, of course, they are also lacking some understanding of you.

There is nothing wrong with a lawyer effectively both using secretaries and paralegals to conspicuously and effectively move your matter forward. However, they are not lawyers, and therefore, cannot make decisions about pleadings and other such important matters. That is not to say they are not used for this purpose and a lawyer who develops a good and effective work relationship with his support staff will very often seek their opinion as to how things are moving along; what else needs to be done and how best to do it. This is an effective sounding board. Now if the people being relied upon are unknown to you, it may be that they are new to your lawyers, on the move again soon, or otherwise impervious, deaf, dumb, and blind your matter and needs. Then where is the A-team? It does not exist. It is outside in the foyer with all of the mahogany. You should know that some law offices go as far as to hire paralegals to design them for maximum overall effect in helping to engage their firm by such trapping designed for impressing clients.

Many years ago, the author had a well-established friend who designed three different rooms for interviewing initial clients one of which was for Caucasian people; one of which was for African American people and one of which was for Latin American people. He uses the resources available to him to maximize effect. There is nothing to suggest that others in large firms do not do likewise.

In meeting with lawyers there are a variety of issues to be determined once the nature of the case has been explored. That is when the "advice" begins. It is origined in your case which should include the lawyer's familiarity with the subject matter; his ability to handle the matter and a detailed history of having handled such matters and who else (boldly asked) does he think in this firm or somewhere else would be better for you?

The desire is to establish an effective group of people to solve your problem and not cater to the personality of the lawyer by ingratiating it with your funds. Many people do not understand how it works and very often there are decisions about whether to sue in state or out of state. Such variables need to be discussed because if they are not the lawyer usually decides to sue for you in his own locale where he gets paid rather than sending you off to some place better when he is then out of a case. You should also understand that the United States Constitution provides that you are entitled to a lawyer of your choosing. That is why when O.J. Simpson assembled his defense team ("A" team), many members were not from California. Ergo: It does not necessarily mean that you have to have a lawyer from your locale handle your matter although it might mean you need a local lawyer to have an out-of-state lawyer admitted to practice specially in your matter *pro hoc vicae* in an association of counsel.

A decision has to be made based on when the matter will be handled in your state as to whether or not you wish to use a lawyer or firm that is in the county of the proceeding or outside the county or even the state. Why? Many lawyers attend the Bar Association functions of their county whether it is golf outings, dinners, or luncheons. This means they have a high level of association with the in-county judges. Many defense firms are so large that they rely upon this principle and assign one of their lawyers on their own to handle a particular judge's courtroom. Therefore, when cases are assigned out by a system known as "the call" by the Administrative Judge at the time your matter is ready for trial, these large firms send a "call lawyer" who then summons the designated firm lawyer who is to present it. Needless-to-say, for weeks before that while the matter progresses through the calendar and the cases before yours dwindle, the "call lawyer" of your firm has already explained to the Assigning Judge that this case belongs to lawyer "X" who is unavailable (or working some place else) and your case is marked "subject to him" thereby assuring that it ends up with him in the courtroom of the judge to which yet another firm lawyer had been internally previously assigned and palpably have obtained some relationship level. They together try to see your matter through, although the well-established lawyer in the designated judge's courtroom may not stay to try it if it cannot be settled. This structure is designed to help you.

The system has been around for some time and is certainly not without its difficulties. It is like a television show of a courtroom. These well-ensconced lawyers are so comfortable in the judge's environment that they know all of the staff by first name, enter his chambers at will, drink his coffee, and eat their cake and cookies. That is not a trick you try if you had only a few cases in front of a judge. Therefore, often the consideration is to get someone who is not from the county particularly if the defense lawyer is likely to be in so well placed in the court's intimate structure than anybody else you seek to hire in your local venue.

Depending upon the nature of the matter, it should be obvious whether it is going to be handled by insurance defense. Very often a judge will pay more deference to an out of state lawyer who has some history of distinction both to appear "fair and impartial" and to disassociate himself from what might become areas of concern experienced by the out-of-state lawyer over whom the court has less apparent control. Also, an out-of-county lawyer is more likely to be outspoken about such matters and the overall concern is to avoid any appearance of impropriety leading to judicial embarrassment.

Chapter Eight

Law Clerks and Former Partners

Sometimes some firms will suggest to you their ability to curry influence with the court. These suggestions include that a former law clerk of the judge works for the firm or so does his relatives or former law partners. Invariably what you are not told is that a well-meaning judge (one who is just not corrupt) will under no circumstance allow a person of relationship or prior intimacy to practice before his court. Therefore, the suggestion of such subtle "influence peddling" is such an odious event that upon the perception of it you can save yourself time as to the rest of the interview and just leave.

There are other suggestions that boldly include those made by some lawyers who are and regard themselves as "fixers." They simply boldly or in oblique terms indicate to you with specific sums of money that they can solve your problem with some direct intervention with the court or its personnel. Obviously, case fixing is a crime, and now again it is time to get up and leave.

Along the lines of the this type of lawyer is sometimes to be found a lawyer who suggests to you how to win your case by creating false evidence, lies, or perjury. However inconceivable, some lawyers actually think this is acceptable. For example, you boldly tell the lawyer you committed a crime because you know that information is privileged, and he cannot reveal it. Then he tells you to persuade your mother, your girlfriend, and two or three other people to testify to an alibi, however false. That alibi is perjury and a lawyer is suborning perjury, which is in itself a crime. When you fall into the hands of a lawyer who is making it obvious to you that a bad case can be made much better by a little perjury then this is the time to put on your sneakers and run out the door.

The dilemma is not as great as you think. A good lawyer can develop by apt questioning a distinct opinion of what occurred without the need for direct confrontational discussion and go on to advise you. It is usually done in the hypothetical form of conversation. In other words, by telling the client that if you were to tell me "X," than I would suggest doing "Y." In this way you have not confessed but still have your answer. The suggestion is not usually errant and usually reveals the ability of the lawyer and not the reverse. However, once you tell any well-established lawyer that you did it, you should not expect him to call you as a witness in denial. He should advise you upfront that he is not going to call you to testify, and at that point you could still be referred to someone else or suffer your own consequences for making an unnecessary disclosure which the lawyer may not have solicited.

Chapter Nine

The Lawyer as a Person In Transference of Identity

The appealability of the lawyer in public by ordinary people needs to be assessed. Many a guilty person has gone free at a jury setting because of pretrial bonding with his lawyer and the lawyer's own positive personality identity. Said differently, if the lawyer appears to the jury acceptable and publicly can relate to you in a positive manner then there is very likely to be a level of transference of identity from the lawyer to you and acceptability by the jury. Said differently, he is "okay then" so you are "okay" too. However, if the lawyer is a cold fish and obviously unable to relate to "John Every Man" then no transference is likely to occur in any positive manner. Rather, the reverse is true.

The art of lawyering is an imprecise one! Many people have gone free or won who should not have because of the lawyer's ability or perception. The reverse is also true. Many a good case has been lost by a stunted cold fish presentation. Any particular lawyer may be a literal genius in his field and his legal knowledge outdoing everyone else's but if he lacks the power of persuasion and can not sing and dance on his feet then your case is out the door of success. A person who is street savvy is more likely to be able to relate professionally (or better than one's opponent in an adversarial system) to the jury at a common level. It needs to be carefully understood that a trial is a one-time event like live television. There is no retaping, film editing, or other "Monday morning quarterbacking" technique that will see you through. The jury has to believe you, and the intellectual influence used on them in your favor is presented and explained one time only. Therefore, the impression that one maintains in this arena of intellectual combat or persuasion is more important and may have much more to do with ultimate success than the ability to read and interpret law books.

Finally, if your lawyer is a cold fish, and you are not, the likelihood of convincing a jury that you have related to each other is strained and can itself lead to distrust of what they are being told by your legal representative. If you are a cold fish too in your personality then you have ever the more need of the warmth of a person who is sophisticated in relating to other people which you may not be able to do. Also, the likelihood of two cold fish getting along for any real sustained period of time is not probable. It is rather predictable that sooner or later you will part company before the final trial event and will have spent your time, effort, and financial resources on a person who did not (and could not) help you from the outset.

In short, to assess these traits you should first rely on your own instinct. Since homo sapiens have walked erect for the last 150 million years, we have all been guided by our human instinct. One's own human instinct is not better or worse than anyone else's. The obvious difference is that our own instinct is best known to each one of us individually, and it is what we have used to guide us in friendships and other important decisions surrounding our human relationships since childhood. Therefore, if there is anything that you feel that you do not like (or you are uncomfortable with) in the proposed lawyer candidate then the only acceptable rule of thumb is to abort at the beginning. A legal undertaking is not an experience in personal rehabilitation. If you come in with the idea that you will change the relationship level even though you have several initial doubts about the person you are becoming involved with then you put yourself down your own primrose lane and should not complain when you find yourself out of luck. It is like playing "Chickey" with yourself. Sooner or later you are going to hit your own wall at a high speed and self-destruct.

As a simple device, when you first meet maybe tell a joke, talk about current events, or talk about political matters. Do you get a joke back? There is nothing wrong with a lawyer who spends some time relating to you but if he cannot talk to you like a person, how do you expect him to talk to a group of stranger jurors on your behalf like a person? If he cannot loosen up then it may well be based on what the lawyer self perceives to be superior education and knowledge. He is experiencing a feeling of inner belief and superiority and that you have not and cannot reach a mutual level of rapport. If that is true of you as a client and he does not want to get to know you better or understand you and your interpersonal needs then it is very unlikely that his art of persuasion will see you through successfully because the jury is likely to conclude that he seems superior to them which will not be a rewarding experience for you in any outcome.

Chapter Ten

Meetings

Sooner or later you are going to schedule appointments and interviews with lawyers. Following engagement there will be a substantial number of ensuing meetings. To understand what is being told to you it is important to bring someone with you who can also recall the circumstances of these discussions. Very often a friend is best or another professional like an accountant, but a smart lawyer will exclude them early for his own reasons of not wishing to be quoted later on, or possibly because the presence of this person opens up attorney-client privilege and may allow the adversary (or those you oppose) to learn what was said back and forth at such meetings. However, preengagement matters may be excluded from such discovery and going in it is best to understand what is being said by having someone else present.

The waiver of the attorney-client privilege is in your control as the client, and it is enough to indicate that you are assuming the risks explained to you.

When you leave such meetings together you should document what you thought was said and reduce it to writing. You will then have a complete understanding both of the relationship and of what you were told (or not told) about the handling of your matter.

You should also early on impress upon the candidate lawyer your desire and willingness to be kept informed of all developments at the various stages of your matter. A lawyer has a professional obligation to keep you "reasonably informed" of your matter as it progresses. This concept lacks clarity. If the law office tells you little or nothing you must set the standard by making it absolutely clear that you want to receive all documents and letters when issued and when received and further to be kept informed of everything that is not a routine telephone call about calendaring or other matters but which certainly include all discussions with experts and your lawyer's adversary. You need to express this initially to determine if your proposed lawyer agrees or is instead responding with "lip service." It is also necessary to call regularly to make certain this is occurring by talking to the support staff. When you find out later, by receiving a letter perhaps, something you did not know, you have to make and reinstruct the lawyer as to how things are to work. You need to be able to recite that this was discussed and agreed upon from the get go at the original discussion. Said differently, if you do not show that you are on top of the ball and support your own matter. Why would anyone else care when there is little or no effort to keep you regularly and reasonably informed?

Chapter Eleven

Jury Selection

Jury selection is a sophisticated matter and has a lot to do with psychological perceptions of the potential jury pool and how they can or might relate to you or your matter. There are people who are experts and professionals in this field. The jury panel list is usually available in advance, and some people hire investigators to learn more especially in a large case or where large corporations are involved. It is a good idea to talk at the outset about the lawyer's prior skills and ability in picking juries and his prior use of experts or willingness to do so in your matter. Jury-selection experts can be expensive, however not using them can lead to a fatal outcome. You are much better off benefitting from their talents to give you the greatest possible advantage in obtaining a positive outcome. The failure to do so (while not necessarily fatal) simply represents a missed opportunity. If your potential lawyer is previously inexperienced in this process then he is expressing that he is content to rely upon his own skills for sorting out the good and bad juror. While such robust confidence in one's own ability is interesting what happens when the other side shows up at the trial with a jury expert and you are sitting there without one? Now you have your lawyer using what are really his own lawyering skills to try and overcome those of an experienced and trained professional.

Jury selection works with experts in two manners. One is to pick the people that will help you and the other is to pick the people who will not help you. Sorting out the second category is much less obvious and is unlikely to be within the lawyer's repertoire when confronted on the other side a jury selection expert. Therefore, it is best to talk about how to proceed at the outset. It is also a good time to find out if the lawyer you are thinking of hiring is some kind of blow heart who thinks his skills and abilities do not need the help of such experts even if others are prepared to use them against him (and you). It is not the greatest turning point in the world of representational selection, but it is a good one to help develop more deeply into how the lawyer thinks about himself and his receptiveness to other viewpoints, including yours. Even if he thinks your idea may come out of right field any elicited response helps reveal his overall ability to consult with you successfully about the interpersonal facts of your matter. If there is rigidity based on the lawyer's own self perception then you have determined rather than the willingness to be open-minded and help that rather you have in a simple interview technique exposed a trait sufficient enough to tell you to stand up and leave.

Chapter Twelve

Big Firm, Little Firm

There is no reason to identify lawyers as more acceptable for your purposes simply because they come from a large or small structure. In prior Chapters we discussed the identity advantage of larger firms to have a greater tendency to be overstated in projecting the advertising or sale of their legal services. Individual small-firm lawyers can easily be similarly adept at such prostetalizing measures.

The concept to keep in mind is that while the lawyer works for the firm (big or little) it is your intention to hire a person who happens to be a member of a law firm. Some clients get carried away because they want to say that they are represented by some large important firm. This mentality of engagement is simply wrong. Many years ago, the author had occasion to be engaged in a patent dispute between a large American enterprise and a large Japanese firm which was accused of infringement. In discussions with their American counsel they indicated that our prominent client would lose in Japan because they had hired the law firm of greatest importance and reputation in Japan. They went on to indicate that this firm had represented War Minister Tojo who led Japan's World War II efforts. Upon immediate reflection the author responded that such confidence was misplaced because Minister Tojo was put to death.

Since you are hiring a lawyer for a new venture, his former public identity is not going to get you very far. If your candidate cannot cut the muster then you are out of luck regardless of the firm. What the difference really is becomes a matter of practical clarity in the engagement itself. Simply put, either in the big firm or little firm you have to make it perfectly plain that you expect the specific lawyer you are hiring (your lawyer) to be handling your matter. Some lawyers you engage in interviews are nothing more than firm "rainmakers," and they pass your matter along to others at their own designation and take financial credit for having turned the matter into the firm. Otherwise they deal with you under the guise that they are handling your matter and may sign pleadings and other documents or letter of which they are virtually unaware. It is not what you want. In the big firm you are likely to be passed down to the section-head lawyer of the involved unit (negligence, family law, or whatever the case may be) who will then assign a junior lawyer who may then even have an associate and paralegal and a whole group of lesser involved people. The net effect is that the lawyer you hired has little or nothing to do with your matter and is certainly most likely not to try it. Actually the "rainmakers" in big firms are usually of a certain age and have long ago given up trying matters or handling them on a daily basis. This is something you need to determine at the outset and make clear your desires and intentions of engagement from the outset interview. Certainly if you are then told that you will be passed along, you need to interview similarly these candidates.

Obviously in the smaller firms of two or three lawyers and in the sole practitioner's office this problem resolves itself or does not exist because there is no one to pass it down to. That does not mean in the smaller firm a lesser person is not able to show up on your matter, but it is less likely to occur as you make it directly known at the outset that it is not what you want.

Finally, in the smaller firm the lawyer you will hire may be complemented by the fact that you do not want anyone else. Accordingly, you have turned it into a positive factor in your relationship. If your requests cannot be met then you (and whoever came with you) ought to be so informed at the outset to aid in the decision process. That does not mean that it is unimportant to consider the other members of the firm either from a brochure or in other available research materials. Obviously, this is easier to do for smaller firms.

Like everyone else lawyers die, get sick, retire, become judges, or win the lottery and quit. Your relationship is not one of involuntary slavery. If this were to happen in your matter while it was progressing some good thought should be given as to the availability of others in the firm to take over. This is best done at the outset than in hindsight, and the same rules apply. You should ask who would take over and put some effort (even if it is minor) into determining if you are going to have a problem with them using your same instinct we earlier discussed in prior chapters.

Chapter Thirteen

Law School Attendance

You are not hiring a law school. Like colleges many talented people go to what is regarded as "lower-tiered" law schools because of issues of finance, school availability, or faculty in residence. If you think you need a "Harvard" or "Philadelphia" lawyer and you are out to get one, you have led yourself astray. Representation by a "B" or "B+" student from a law school you never heard of would be better than that of a "C" student from "Harvard". Believe that there are "C" students in every laws school, including Harvard and Stanford.

At the practical levels of the practice of law, no one really cares where a lawyer went to school; however, bear in mind that there are subtle differences. If my matter is in New Jersey and the involved lawyer went to an out-of-state law school he is less likely to be involved in the climate of the legal community historically and more likely to be convinced if he is "Harvard" or "Yale" that he is superior to those collegaues from "Rutgers" or "Seton Hall." If someone is tooting where they went to school then their need to puff is itself a negative circumstance. Telling you where they went to law school[3] (as though you would be impressed) is a self-sell technique of little value except to reveal a palpable negative personality trait sufficient for you to leave.

Moreover, in the example of New Jersey law school attendance set forth the lawyer will see five years of graduating classes including the two ahead of his and the two behind his. This is real exposure as to who will be in the legal community to provide resources and contacts and forms the legal pool that most judges will emerge. Therefore, the hometown (i.e.: home-state law degree) while perhaps not as publicly treasured may in the long run have more practical value. This is a factoid to develop especially if you are being puffed about, your candidate's fancy prior law school environment.[4]

---

3   E.g. "When I was at Harvard Law School . . . ."

4   It is easier to determine where most people went to law school especially if the law firm is large enough to have any literature or firm membership catalogues either on the Internet or in their office on display.

Chapter Fourteen

Advertising

There are several ways to find a lawyer. One method is to ask friends, but without a legal background or hands-on legal exposure how can they really be of help? Another method is to succumb to advertised business firms which tell you that they will provide you with legal referrals. These agencies by and large do not deeply investigate either the firms or individuals that register, but rather charge a fee to the lawyer for getting on the list to enjoy the opportunity of being sent business which they could not otherwise obtain. Another likely solution is to engage lawyers who blitz on television, the Internet, and newspapers for business. Considering the long history of the legal profession you should be aware that advertising for only the last two decades is professionally acceptable which in the author's opinion is more motivated by business considerations than by professional distinction. Obviously, those people who are willing to or who can spend the money to get their cowboy faces on television are going to outstrip everybody else in business getting. Accordingly, a profession has denigrated itself into becoming a swarmy business environment by the profit of such techniques. Many people would disagree and are free to do so, but it is certainly unquestionable that he who does the most advertising is going to get the most referrals and starts. This conclusion is a simple matter of common sense wherein the uninitiated or lazy think it is sufficient to hire the first lawyer they see based on some advertisement or referral list.

When the author's father joined the Bar in New Jersey there were approximately 4,000 lawyers. When the author joined, there were about 8,000 lawyers. Upon best calculation, there are approximately 80,000 lawyers now in this one state alone! This is a big ocean to swim successfully in terms of selection. However, people did not hire Abraham Lincoln because he wore a cowboy hat but because he had a very good reputation. Reputation for legal success is the best criteria and not advertising money.

In terms of determining reputation and ability overall, there are different criteria by which to be guided including the references from other people who had a successful outcome (assuming that is what really happened rather than they just got "some money"). It is difficult to know if you are being told accurate legal war stories by others.

Lawyers have trouble hiring other lawyers, so why should it be any easier for you? Therefore the necessity for this book.[5] Very often big business will engage outside counsel for the purposes of engaging, interviewing and selecting counsel. In short, the selecting attorney is acting as a consultant. The exercise of locating counsel for people in the public realm is an emerging concept. If you calculate the likelihood of outcome and the amount of money required to be paid out (either on a contingent or hourly fee basis) the overall concept of engagement of a professional consultant to guide in the selection process is a comparatively minor expense and likely justified. When these consultants are lawyers themselves they may also be experienced in the art of negotiation of the fee that can lead to enhanced savings far in excess of the consultation fees. It is a positive concept.

---

5   You might find this book unique in its focus and openness. Could it be such knowledge or perception is known only to a select few who have elected to disclose it? Will this publication enhance the popularity of the author in the legal community? Do the concepts put forward help the law person and as such are they a contribution to the public good?

Certainly you can ask some friend who is a lawyer for a referral, but what you really need to do is stay informed and hands-on yourself. The lawyer friend is able to refer the matter to what is known as a "certified trial attorney" and then receive back one-third of the fee generated or whatever their agreement becomes. Accordingly, he is not sending you to the "best and brightest" but rather to the lawyer to whom he regularly refers matters and who he knows will pay him. Many people who accept such referrals get to be a payment problem later on so "the devil you know is better that the devil you don't know" and the referral goes to an established friend rather than to whomever may be best for you. Accordingly the use of a lawyer friend for referral of who else to engage is not the best resource over the use of a lawyer who is a consultant who will examine the matter involved; the locale; compose a list of interviews and attend the same should you so elect.

There is another difficult caution against the use of casual attorney friends for referrals which is many of the people who receive them have extremely large practices but not necessarily large law firms. Some will decline a matter based on the fact that they do not feel it is of value to them especially if they have to pay a forwarding fee. They might be right for your matter but the cost of a one-third "shave and a haircut" on their fee has put them off.

An opportunity has been lost![6] in consultant issues. This means if they do not feel they can settle they can settle the case for $1 million or more or some unauthorized figure they have garnered in another's mind then they are not available. On the other hand many of the lawyers with extremely large practices take on so many matters on referral (in part both because they are getting a lesser fee due to the referral) but have established large internal inner-office structures to keep busy that matters are taken with the intention of settling quickly and with maximum income and reduce time, effort and expense. This practice however odious is calculated to make you a member of a flock of clients rather than someone of significant individual importance. Remember that once you settle your case, complaining later about what you got or didn't get is likely to be barred as a legal malpractice claim. Lawyers will settle your case (big or small) for whatever you are willing to take. If they can talk you into something cheap and

---

6   So then you might opine why engage a consultant who should also help you negotiate the fee! The answer becomes the first job is to locate a good lawyer candidate pool and the second is then to resolve fees. A lawyer might agree to 25% or 30%, but you are still ahead and most likely have easily covered the cost of your consultant and still come out well ahead. Also, you might reach, through the consultant, a hybrid solution where the lawyer gets 20% if he settles with your approval the matter before suit, for example in the negligence area, or agrees to an hourly fee reduction acceptable to you. In this manner, the lawyer's hourly rate is negotiated down which still puts you well ahead and still saves him from paying out to your referring lawyer friend his referral fee of one-third of the lawyer's fee.

easy at the beginning then that what is most likely to occur. If there is an insurance policy and they "get the policy" although there might be claims to pursue it is not likely to occur.[7]

---

7   Several years ago there was a published New Jersey Supreme Court opinion about a woman who sought a divorce from a successful husband. In having taken the case the lawyer in six short weeks without discovery of the husband's individual assets in a long-term marriage was able to get her $20 million as she early on settled her case. Shortly thereafter she went to the Country Club and a friend asked her how she made out and she expressed her glee over $20 million in such a short time. Her friend advised her that her husband's assets exceeded $100 million and she had lost out on nearly twice the amount she got. Quick may not be best.

Chapter Fifteen

Lawyers As Guarantors

The legal profession is an imprecise one. No lawyer can or should guarantee any result. If someone is whipping you up at the interview that you suffered a great injustice and they will vindicate your cause getting you both money and vengeance ("a pound of flesh") then you should leave.

The reason you need to deliberate yourself about selecting a lawyer is to avoid the puff and sales techniques. Even when things are going well there can be a change in the law or all sorts of procedural curve balls thrown successfully which have the ability to strike you out of court. "To be forewarned is to be forearmed," and to protect yourself at the outset including from any lawyer assures or guarantees an outcome in the murky area of the law. Now that is not to say that somehow legal matters are not highly predictable in outcome determination, but they can still be lost in the eleventh hour. For example, it is highly likely to obtain a positive outcome if you want to hire a lawyer to disinherit a child. This is not a litigatory circumstance in which you have to always consider that the legal playing ground has 54 cards, two of which are Jokers. Nevertheless, there are still no guarantees because the act itself may be improperly scribed or not competitively executed at execution and still ends up in costly estate litigation which could well be lost.

Chapter Sixteen

Specialty Lawyers

The obvious circumstance is that some lawyers are better educated and trained in certain specialty areas than others. For example, some lawyers may indicate that they do patent work of a general nature. This does not mean that they are any less qualified than anyone else to design a patent or design around an existing patent which is what patent law accepts and inspires. However, assume that your patent deals with the applicability of some aspect as to the flow of surface waters and the hydrology involved in the design of the patent. Patent protection comes both from uniqueness and the ability to deepen as much as possible the breath of the patent claims so that your patent will remain viable and unchallenged for the 20 years available rather than having someone else simply design around it by making a better mousetrap.

Accordingly, if you were to find a patent attorney who also had a background as a hydrogenist (rather than as a criminal defense attorney or divorce attorney) then wouldn't you be likely better proceeding with him? In patent law the attorney-client relationship is not as important although obviously if you cannot relate to each other at the outset do not move forward. However, in certain specialties where a specific education or background is important there is still the need to convince the "other side" of your legal position and its merit. Thus a developed relationship with your patent attorney who might need to persuade the Patent Office of the significant nature of your claims remains of utmost importance. The prior standards are the same, and if you can not get along even despite talent or education it would be appropriate to find someone of similar qualifications who can relate to you. Working relationship level still remaining the bedrock of any engagement.

Chapter Seventeen

Insurance Matters

Insurance policies differ. If you are policy entitled to insurance coverage lawyers, they will be assigned to you by your insurance company. Usually they come from an available panel. If you are not pleased with them, you should immediately contact your agent and express your concerns and your desire to interview others who may be available from the panel with whom you are better suited to proceed.

When working with a lawyer initially prior to any insurance-coverage lawyer assignment (and always when you are being sued) you should make inquiry at any interview as to whether or not you might be covered under a policy of insurance available to you. Finding and employing such coverage also allows you to make separate decisions including whether to be represented by the insurance company attorney in defense of the matter and by private counsel of your choosing in the bringing of any counterclaims or affirmative claims that you might have. This gives you fuller legal resources and the ability to have a double-headed tag team if done properly. Moreover, insurance lawyers are there to provide a defense and may not caution you about affirmative claims you have or may have which they are either unwilling or unlikely to bring because it is not part of their insurance engagement for which they are paid by your insurance company. Normally, insurance companies will not pay for the bringing of your affirmative claims unless absolutely convinced that it is necessary for the defense issues to prevail.

Chapter Eighteen

Bar Association Referrals

Most counties in the various states have Bar Associations which enjoy referral programs. Mostly, the names provided are those of young attorneys seeking business who are out on their own and otherwise unestablished yet in their reputations. Experience aside, there is nothing objectionable about these younger lawyers. Rather, you are likely to meet a warmer group who are more interested in pursuing your matter to help establish themselves and their skills (rather than for money alone). Some of them are highly talented, hardworking and may already be better than they think. It is like plucking a diamond out of the ruff at a Kimberly, South Africa mine. Your case helps polish their skills and reputation, but the intrinsic value is already there in ability. Conversely, you can also fall on a fool who happened to garner a law degree but is otherwise not suited. That is why you need to rely upon your own intellectual instincts.

Moreover, you should also be aware that the Bar Associations do little or nothing to check the qualifications and experience of the lawyers who register except perhaps as to whether they are actually in good standing and have a license to practice. They also charge the attorney who accepts such a referral matter for some fee (which is modest and not of importance to the selection process) but you should be aware of it. Said differently, when you are calling a Bar Association (rather than using a consulting service) they are really doing little or nothing to guide you. They are likely only to provide you with the referral list of the people practicing in your designated case area without telling you anything more. Indeed, they are constrained from doing so by the perception that it would be wrong to prefer one member of the referral panel over another. They will not become involved (like a consultant) in helping you further designate which one to choose or in matters concerning the lawyer's fees and recommendations.

Chapter Nineteen

Directories
General & Specific

There are many outside sources for determining the availability of attorneys in your area. Most of these can be found in law libraries maintained by State and County Bar Associations. Most states also have very substantial law libraries open to the public most usually, at least in the state capitols and also on the campus and state law schools if they exist. Gaining entrance to these facilities requires some disclosure of identity but it is not particularly difficult and the design is to try and maintain it for lawyers, law students and public benefit. They are something likely to be used even by judges for reference matters including statutory history and development and also particularly by Legislators and their legal staffs.

Within the libraries upon polite request an experienced and degreed Law Librarian should be well willing to help you find the materials that you need. This does not mean that they are going to read it for you or interpret it but rather simply tell you where it is so you can do so.

The most exhausting source that exists for lawyers is <u>Martindale-Hubbell</u> which is available both in hard copy at most every public law library and also on CD Rom. It certainly may be obtained for private purchase by contacting the publisher.[8] The document provides the identity of virtually all lawyers actively practicing throughout these United States as well as in various foreign countries and their so-called legal "rating." However, the rating determined is not particularly relevant because basically it involves a variety of internal decisions made by Martindale-Hubbell as well as soliciting information from other lawyers who may know the individual being then "rated". These ratings should not guide you.

The publication will also tell you about various law firms and if the lawyer revealed is practicing in one which has taken out an advertisement within the publication. Thus, you can turn to such a placement which in large firms can run on for pages and actually research fairly well where the lawyer you have identified

---

8   See bibliography.

fits into the firm's structure and what his curriculum vitae history is which normally reveals areas of practice.

In using this tool by yourself (should you so elect) you may easily become confused since the amount of material is vast. By way of example, let's say you are from Baltimore, Maryland and you and your wife were in a car accident in Cleveland, Ohio. Most likely your lawsuit will have to be brought in Cleveland because the is where the accident occurred and you may have no state court "jurisdiction" over the persons you feel are responsible except where they live in Ohio.

Using Martindale-Hubbell you locate attorney "X" and look up his firm reference. Although he is of interest to you in your negligence matter you note that he sat on Bar Association sections and published a few articles on matrimonial law. This does not seem to be the person for your negligence matter. However, while reading through his firm's directory you note other lawyers who are members of the American Trial Lawyer's Association and who have sat on committees or written about negligence concepts. You may also find that the firm does automobile defense work in which event they may not be likely interested in a plaintiff's matter. However, you might also find more positively that although in Cleveland there is a member of the firm who went to The Johns Hopkins University in Baltimore and The

University of Maryland Law School thereby giving them roots in your locale and perhaps a friendlier environment for you being a substance distance. This might well be a lawyer of interest for you to contact even though their firm might not do this type of work. It may well be that there is some other local connection that can be explored to a positive conclusion where you get the advice you need. Certainly a negligence defense attorney can tell you who is pretty good in their negligence field in plaintiff's work and it means little or nothing to them except as a courtesy and in aid of serving the public.

It is necessary to remain perfectly clear. These reference journals while they provide a lot of information do not necessarily become easy for the layperson to interpret. The book is basically written by lawyers for lawyers and you can be certain Martindale-Hubbell has a well trained editorial staff of people who include lawyers. It is the law firm who writes their own placement and you can be sure that they consider it to be part of their advertising budget. It is difficult or impossible for the layperson to interpret (sic: very likely misinterpret) what is actually to be found in the listing. You may well see that a particular lawyer is on a lot of committees; has written a lot of articles (or had his support staff of subordinates and paralegals write them under his name) and he looks pretty good to you. The truth is he's supposed to because it is advertising and how would you know better? There are so many committees for lawyers to join that it is virtually impossible to designate which ones are of any particular value. For example, you may see an "important" lawyer has all sorts of appealing credentials, publications and committee associations. You are impressed. You may see another lawyer either in sole practice or a small firm who lists very little personal historical distinction except having been a law professor and a member of The American Law Institute. Since the space dedicated to him is substantially smaller than the ones found early about the more impressive lawyer, your instinct is to avoid the apparently less distinguished attorney. What you do not realize is that being an adjunct law professor under various circumstances is a matter of very apt professional distinction compared to some seemingly "important" attorney who may or may not be doing much of anything on his own. What you do not understand is that the candidate visiting professor has only listed limited criteria such as The American Law Institute because to the experienced attorney reading Martindale-Hubbell he does not have to show any further distinctions. One is enough! What lawyers know is that The American Law Institute is limited to 1,500 lifetime members and arrived at only because you are literally in the intellectual top cream of the legal profession. The members help write the laws adopted by Congress and most states for ultimate statutory authority. They are not so very distinguished because they serve on every mundane state or local Bar Association committee but because they serve this one resource which alone outstrips all others. Within the limited membership only 600 are lawyers and 900 are judges which means that you are talking about a distinction far above average which fitters down to about twelve such people of distinction state by state. How are you to know without someone to guide you? The result is that you were able to find the right reference materials but not successfully interpret them for best use. However, this alone by yourself may be a good starting point to locate a lawyer in Ohio perhaps from Baltimore who will help you in your search.

There are other publications of interest. For example, there are many which discuss how to sue lawyers and even judges (a far more difficult undertaking but one which is becoming even more popular in our society). Obviously, even today most lawyers are not going to sue other professional members, especially judges. They feel they do not need this work or that it will otherwise taint them as an outsider or maverick. Certainly that is their decision. On the other hand, a few lawyers are still deeply involved in due process; constitutional and civil rights; and compelling issues of freedom recognizing that everybody is entitled to adequate counsel under the Sixth Amendment of the United State Constitution. These are powerful lawyers who generally are already publically distinguished.

Understanding that a lawyer's training is supposed to alter the way you think socially (and does) it is important to understand that appearances of possible recrimination for unpopular issues are meaningless to the lawyer who seeks the need to undertake such matters. These are the lawyers who may well undertake your matter and likely handle it in a diligent and competent manner because they are not given to light or casual undertakings. If they say they "are in," then you can be fairly well certain that they are.[9]

---

9   Everybody has heard of the <u>Miranda</u> warnings. Namely at the time of arrest "be silent or it will be used against you, and if you want a lawyer, you may have one. Few members of the public know or understand that after <u>Miranda</u> came <u>Escabido</u>. In that case decided by the United States Supreme Court (following up on their decision in Miranda) it was apparent that Danny Escabido in a premeditated manner set out to kill his brother-in-law and was successful. He was given the <u>Miranda</u> instructions at the time of arrest but the Supreme Court decided that it did not like how he was given them or the cirucmstances surrounding it. Danny Escabido (known murder) was set free by the grey-haired very senior Justices of our United States Supreme Court with a lot of education and distinction. What this means is everything is not what it seems and having a lawyer who is experienced in Due Process or other hard tact legal issues may well be better.

Chapter Twenty

Yellers & Screamers

Lawyers are strong willed like stallions and very often they need to be. This is not in defense of an attorney who lacks culture or cooth but impoliteness is very often indigenous to the type of person who seeks a career in the law. It is this for the outsider layperson to at least appreciate the stress of the law upon all practitioners in terms of the dedication and work effort involved (if the lawyer elects to put it forth). It is best to know the nature of the beast with whom you will have to deal down the road, especially should their fangs suddenly appear.

At the outset there is no doubt that a young lawyer start in the legal mailroom. Obviously when reviewing the credibility of a lawyer if you observe that he has been an editor of the Law Review of the law school and has clerked for a federal or state court Justice or some other Appellate Court then you know at least other professionals were well regarding his quality and integrity early on. The reason for this is that a law school education can properly frame your legal mindset but has absolutely little or nothing to do with the practical aspects of practice itself or otherwise earning a living. This is something you learn on your own (or not). Also many law professors feel it is not necessary to teach this because many lawyers once educated go on to business or other careers and it is not necessary to instruct them further on how to stand on their own two feet economically. Finally, law professors are not exactly the best-paid individuals in the profession. If anything they are at the lower end of the spectrum well behind judges and very often earn less than people right out of law school get in big Wall Street firms at a time they know little or nothing about the practice of law. Therefore, it would make little sense for these people to instruct students about how to earn a living by actually practicing law which full-time law professors do not do. This does not mean they cannot be involved in matters by actually serving as consultants or experts and although they may be available for such work they are more likely to refer you to their friends and associates.

Relating back to the lawyer's structure from the fledgling emergence from the law school eggshell you have entered a structure controlled from the top. You respond to more senior members of the firm whether associates or junior partners or big bosses and you are obligated to work yourself to death with fear in your heart. Either you are going to make partner or you will not. You also have commitments outside the practice including lawyers' wives and children who suffered perhaps through long years of education and who rely on you to make it all worthwhile.

Finally as your career climbs and you stay long enough to actually become a member of the firm (rather than simply an employee) you are subject to odious firm meetings during which firm policy is dictated by the big bosses. You are told what you should earn for yourself and family and why it should not be what you thought despite what you perceive to be your competitive apparent success. You do not understand how long it is going to take before you become a big boss in our capitalistic society and get to live off of the sweat of lesser attorneys. You also may not like the criteria or direction of being told how and when to resolve a matter that you felt could have been exploited better for the client even though you understand economic considerations of the law firm and its rulers guide this direction. Now as you begin to move forward as a full-fledged practicing lawyer you have gotten a heavy case load; a series of commitments outside the practice which are greater now than before; exposure to judges who order you into trial (ready or not); and still sitting above you is a group of senior law partners flinging what you think is mud at you from a top-heavy structure. It is enough to make you explode!

The yeller and screamer syndrome does not mean that the lawyer is unfit to conduct your matter. It does reveal that there is substantial pressure on the lawyer which might effect the availability of time for you realistically and presents other issues of concern. Now if the lawyer simply has lost it (hopefully temporarily) and is otherwise vile and cruel particularly to his own subordinates in your presence then out come the track shoes again.

It is still not as clear cut as it seems. A good lawyer knows that at the end if everything else does not work that he is going to have to try your case or otherwise present your matter. If he can not do so appropriately from a sustained distance while you are in the witness chair then the likelihood of success diminishes greatly. Accordingly at the very beginning in deciding themselves if they want your matter a smart lawyer explores around the fringes of your own intellect. He is trying to determine what makes you tick; what are your actual intellectual and verbal abilities; what are your listening and answering skills; how deep is your understanding of your own matter; how common is your goal and at what point do you boil over and what triggers it. You need to recall that any interview is a two-way street. The lawyer may think you have the greatest case in the world but if you can not bring it home then it is of not particular value because he can not testify for you. Accordingly, you may be also addressed in a way which you feel is too high-styled or otherwise inappropriate but it may well have on occasion from a smart and sophisticated lawyer's mind an apt purpose. Therefore, just because you are being interrogated (although it may be uncomfortable) does not mean that your matter is not being well explored. You need to be guided to use your best instinct as to what is actually occurring. Is it unacceptable behavior or is it instead appropriate in the meeting of two strangers in a common goal? If you decide that the interview technique was appropriate then you probably found a smart individual to help but of course you need to discuss it with whomever you brought with you.

Chapter Twenty-One

Lying and Other Sleaze

However incredible it may seem, at an initial interview or shortly thereafter a discussion with your lawyer might lead to the topic of how either to gather up evidence in your matter in an unacceptable fashion or to otherwise tailor your testimony and those of your witnesses in a manner which is clearly not truthful. Should this come up: leave, leave, leave. This is another reason why you have brought someone with you so that you are not uncertain about what you are being told. Accordingly, if the suggestion is to throw out documents or otherwise get together with a group of people to lie on your behalf as witnesses then you have started down a road of self-destruction having little or nothing to do with your case. This is certain to substantially impact the future of your matter and its outcome. Many a good case has been dismissed because of such sleaze by a defense lawyer's ability to out it and bend over your lawyer or you to the point where you have no choice but exposure or quitting your case pursuits. Such a negative result would have been impossible if the wrong road was not taken. If you are not sure about what you are being told and whether it is proper or not then ask.

Most states have a disciplinary history of its Bar members and most of this information is available online. Although the topic can become controversial, attorney discipline is not necessarily a proof that a lawyer is not suited for your needs. You have to decide yourself by assessing your perception of the lawyer. However, if the lawyer already pulled some real trick of dishonesty or lack of integrity he would have been disbarred. After decades of practice it is a little bit difficult to remain in a perfect state and if you do, it may be that as a lawyer you have no real "get up and go" on your client's behalf. Said differently, the legal system is run by lawyers who decide which side ("good guy – bad guy" it is perceived that a lawyer fits in. Good guy or not, if you have made your career defending people who are not apparently acceptable to society (murderers and drug dealers) then you can expect like Roy Cohn, Esq. to be the subject of professional enmity and to have professional complaints lodged against you whether they have merit or not. Sooner or later such a spitball might stick to the wall. This is especially true if you have made your career in part by suing lawyers and judges. What did you think would be the comeuppance? Accordingly, just because a lawyer has been determined to have had some technical violation does not mean that he may not be virulent enough for your needs. The real issue is how do you assess him and not how did others before your own topic developed.

Chapter Twenty-Two

Fees and Commitments

In many states except to set the circumstances of hourly services, many established attorney-client relationships are already regulated by statutes or Rules of Court. Again in New Jersey by way of example lawyers are required to use fee structures in documents approved and promulgated by the State Supreme Court. Accordingly virtually all lawyers will be handing you the same approved retainer agreements. (See Appendix).

There are many issues that you do not understand most likely going in. Although the fee structure is regulated, for example, in negligence matters, a certified trial attorney (as earlier discussed) can remit up to one-third of the fee to the forwarding attorney. He can likewise share fees with the lawyer who referred him your case. To earn their fee the referring lawyer need do nothing more than forward the matter. Very often they will attend earlier interview sessions to make sure the matter is signed up in the law office of their choosing in order to ensure getting their forwarding referral fee. The legal system permits this. This is why it may be better to find a lawyer on your own or prefer to use a consultant.

A legal engagement consultant does not give legal advice about your matter. They are helping guide you in your selection. In doing so, they have very right on your behalf to discuss the overall fee structure including indicating that although they may be able to accept a referral fee especially from a certified trial lawyer that they would rather see these monies go back to you. This does not mean that you should only seek out certified trial attorneys or their firms. Perhaps a non-certified trial attorney will be as receptive to the topic and is usually older and does not see the need to be a certified practitioner for reasons of ongoing education of skills that they have already developed.

Some of the most experienced practitioners at the law have resources beyond your imagination from the skills of practicing law or other business relationships that came along the pathways of their career. Senator John Edwards, Esq. of North Carolina is such an example and the wide extent of his assets are well known. He is certainly not alone in the past. They include such people as Melvin Belli (the King of Torts) and in Texas, Racehorse Haines. As far back as ten years ago or more it was remorsed that Racehorse Haines would not even interview a case to see if he would consider taking it without being paid a half million dollars for the interview process. Whether true or not, it shows the value of some lawyers and many of them are willing to adjust their fees on your behalf if properly negotiated in a non offensive manner.

Assume by way of example you have been in a car accident and unfortunately injured. Happily the policy of insurance because you were hit by a commercial vehicle is large enough to be $1 million. The fee schedule if you got the full policy might be as much as $200,000.00 or more for your law firm in fees. The referring lawyer would receive $60,000-$70,000 or more for bringing you through the mahogany doors. By negotiation this sum of potential referral money might be partially or fully returned to your overall which is obviously a fraction of whatever you may have spent on engaging a consultant to accomplish this successful result. Similarly true, if your legal bill is going to be non contingent and on an hourly basis you might be better off spending a modest sum of money on a consultant with the foreknowledge that when successful multiples of this sum will be returned to you. This becomes even more important because very often negligence awards are generally considered not to be taxable income and the sums of money to be received tax free become even more valuable especially if you can deduct from them any consultant fees.

There are other subordinate considerations other than your own direct legal fees because you will be responsible in the retainer agreement for paying these indirect costs. These include experts and the overall cost of litigation. You might think that the lawyer should pay for this but generally under the Rules of Professional Practice it is not possible. In some instances it is regarded as championary which generally prohibits the lawyer from funding the litigation. That is not to say that some lawyers may not agree to advance certain fees as encouragement for you to engage them. Whether or not this is acceptable professionally voices the particular matter but such funding lackness is also a lawyer's sales technique. Why would one lawyer do so when mostly all others would not? Obviously, in order to be hired. Generally the cost of experts can be substantial and most cases will require you to fund them from your own resources at the outset. A good legal practitioner will be less likely to be willing to advance them.

You should make certain in your negotiation of the fees and other retainer matters that all engagement of experts are made with your approval and knowledge including particularly their fee structure and their payment. Many of these experts are used time and again by the same lawyer and have become their friends. It should not surprise you that after your case they will need to use them still again and again and again. Your case may well be the opportunity for the lawyer to recommend again his own expert friends because he needs him in another case which may not be yet funded or well funded. It can become slick. On the other hand, these experts may elect to charge thousands of dollars for pretrial standby time although they never appear in court and the matter is settled on the courthouse steps while taking large sums of $7,500.00 to $15,000.00 for such no-show episodes of little or no real value to you at the bitter end. If you do not have a clear understanding as to these types of expenses you will find later if challenged that the court allows the lawyer on review to dole out these monies without any prior understanding, writing or agreement. If you are going to pay $15,000.00 for an expert doctor who never showed up for standby while he is playing golf or otherwise working, you should certainly know about it and insist on some criteria to prove that there is no double-dipping. If you do not control it at the beginning, you will not be able to do so later on. If you are getting yourself into such unchartered waters and start bringing up such topics at the interview, you may well find that you have turned off a lawyer who could have helped you and would have if such topics had been more artfully plead by a consultant. It is a little bit more difficult for the lawyer being interviewed to explain why he would not or should not allow you to participate in the full understanding of the use of such expert witnesses and what their fee rates and other stand-by requirements might be. However, when done alone by you the lawyer may conclude that this provokes some type of overall negative impression of you which will not foster him to be allowed to be engaged by you because the relationship will only get worse. Any engagement still also remains a matter of the lawyer's perceptions or misperceptions also.

Chapter Twenty-Three

Loans, Advances & Recovery

Short sale in advance of the cause of action itself are sometimes suggested to a potential client. In a brief period of interview time the lawyer may have determined that your case has an ultimate substantial value and a high likelihood of success. For example, you have been struck from behind by a Fed Ex truck at a high speed while stopped at a red light in broad daylight and sustained serious and permanent injuries. Your matter is obviously a winner. Now you are told about your need for medical experts and to finance the litigation and that the cost of it could be $20,000; $30,000; or $40,000 or more in such expenses to "work it up." You very well at the same time may not be told that because of the serious nature of the permanent injuries and the obvious negligence that occurred in your accident that the lawyer may obtain the policy of $1 million in a very short period of time of a few months by working through an adjuster and that no lawsuit might be necessary. Unless you have negotiated the retainer agreement as to what happens if the case settles before any suit is filed, you have not successfully negotiated it. You pay the full fee that you agreed upon whether the matter was difficult or protracted or not. Some lawyers will suggest to you that since you cannot finance the litigation but because they still want to help you that they will arrange for you to borrow the money that you need to do so or arrange for you to sell your outcome in advance at a discount and get paid for your matter now. What they may not tell you is that they are involved in the enterprise willing to do so either by receiving fees, commissions or outright ownership in such businesses. Incredibly some of these arrangements are acceptable within the legal system. Whether they should be or not is a topic for another day, but if put in this position your overall consideration should be to go someplace else where you are not considered a chattel but rather a person with injuries that need to be addressed outside of a shakedown.

Finally, the retainer agreement (although not a financial term) should and must contain the concept that your matter cannot be settled by the lawyer without your specific authority in advance. This requires the lawyer to disclose to you (as well he should in any event) all offers and other financial matters affecting your outcome. As incredible as it may seem a lawyer you engage has every right to settle your matter. Once your lawyer agrees to do so and this is able to be demonstrated by letter or other evidence the retained authority which you have given is sufficient to allow the settlement made without your knowledge to be enforced despite your later day non approval. Therefore all of a sudden you find that a large matter has settled for a sum that is unacceptable to you but still it fuels the lawyer's ability to obtain his legal fee and just places you in an argument level for which you may have no ongoing desire. Protect yourself at the outset by specific refinement of the retainer arrangement or determine that you cannot agree with the candidate lawyer and move on.

Chapter Twenty-Four

Non-Legal Lawyer Assets

During the earlier chapters we have discussed substantially the legal qualifications, experience, and other criteria of the candidate lawyer crucial in the selection process. This does not limit the criteria of choice which is to be tailored on a case by case basis. It is not a broad spectrum issue like attorney diligence or competence.

Assume that in putting together your A-team that you are a director and producer of a film that will either bomb at the box office or be successful. You say when to shoot and what the camera angles are with the pitch of light. These are really like the same types of discussions that you have (and need to have) in the handling of your matter. A lawyer is duty-bound to follow your direction and advice so long as it is not illegal or unethical. The problem is that most clients do not understand their own full authority and remain passive invariably rather than proactive. This does not mean that you should become bossy in legal areas that you do not understand, but if you have developed a rapport with your lawyer than it should lead to a sufficient mutual understanding allowing your real input.

Among these film production type considerations become the obvious and subtle (and often non-legal) avenues of persuasion available. These are not very difficult to determine. If you allege that you have been sexually abused by discriminatory statements in the workplace from men then psychologically it might make sense for you to consider hiring a female attorney experienced in the area. It would be more likely to assume that such a person could express a sufficient sense of female-identity outrage with you as a client to bring your victory home. This would not necessarily be true if you were with a patriarch or an elderly balding cold fish "big shot lawyer" in some large law firm. It becomes apparent in these circumstances that you are just another client and there is no female-identity outrage transference.

Likewise if you are charged with a serious crime and you elect to have a lawyer that you could pay less but who was otherwise meek and partially tongue tied may allow the jury to conclude that in their own good conscience that they can find you guilty and go home early. This result is because you are perceived also to be meek and acceptable to such short-shrift. When your matter requires a large lion who roars to protect either your liberty or your assets you certainly should make sure that you have one who can sing and dance with his mouth and brain in public on his feet spontaneously.

Racial identity is far more difficult. Assuming you are accused of a hate crime by writing unpleasant racial words on the side of a church of African Americans. It would be a hard defense to sell by showing up with an African-American attorney. Sometimes you go too far in staging and the jury (like the movie goers) may think that your film was poorly cast and not believable. Ask yourself: Could Leonard Nimoy after an association of so many years of Dr. Spock effectively play James Bond? Can Sean Connery play Dr. Spock? You might say to the contrary that these are characters developed over the years, so the inquiry is not fair. However, the obvious is also true. You are either white or you are not. You are either female or male. We have been playing these roles since the beginning of time which has little or nothing to do with a lawyer's ability. Obviously, once you have made your decision of character type staging you can then set about trying to find someone within the designated group with sufficient skills and dedication to your matter. This is neither sexist nor silly but rather betokens the fullest consideration to the casting for your ultimate presentation of your matter. Getting the best A-team together is not some type of causal parlor game but should be viewed as preparation for a war game.

For decades in earlier America the mantra from virtually all ethnic groups was to find what they considered to be "a good Jewish lawyer." The why of it involves the myths surrounding the mental ability of the Jewish people and their history of their dedication of knowledge to the biblical law leading to a conclusion that they were better educated or naturally gifted in the areas of understanding of law. They were known to be highly verbal and well motivated for money. Nowadays, most ethnic groups have seen fit to seek out lawyers of their own kind. Although I do not think we should betoken a return to the mentality that everyone should have a Jewish lawyer. The mindset of choosing a lawyer only of your own ethnic background should also be rejected. Take the lawyer who is best for you.

Many sophisticated companies and individuals were historically drawn to lawyers of Jewish origin because in the early inception of the legal community in America (certainly between the 1920s and 1930s) the Jewish community enjoyed a very substantial disproportionate entrance to and involvement in the legal community, courts, and court system. This may be difficult initially to fully understand. Consider however that the Jewish population in America currently is only about one-half of one percent (.05%) and was pre-World War II below that. Nevertheless their infusion into the legal society was vastly far greater percentagewise, and therefore they stood out more and were perceived as the winning group. In large dimension the Irish have now infiltrated substantially disproportionately but that is not a reason either just to get an Irish lawyer. Therefore, in staging, you have to avoid the misperception that just because Johnny Depp might be regarded as the sexiest man alive that he is right for your film.

Chapter Twenty-Five

Rules of Conduct

Many retainer agreements delineate the professional lawyer and client obligations back and forth in text. You have already been cautioned to read them most carefully and to take them away from the place of initial interview for negotiation once reviewed by you and/or with your consultant. Nevertheless, you must bear in mind that from these agreements there are rules of conduct that guide the lawyer professionally in handling your matter. These rules of conduct try to assure professional integrity, honesty, and competence and are not multiple-choice guidelines only for the lawyer to accept or reject. Rather, they are to be religiously followed in full. They include disciplinary rules as well as other rules guiding the professional relationship. They are easy to find and actually are available state to state on the Internet or from the publisher of the Court Rules which also discuss procedurally how to get in and out of court. While potentially complicated for the layperson they are an invaluable source of information, such as time limits and other valuable information. They are well indexed and (depending upon the publisher) include a variety of law after each rule that will help you interpret it. Indeed many a person who has become involved in legal but cannot find or afford a lawyer has been required to resort to being their own counsel and to obtaining and reviewing these materials. If they can do it then why can't you? Why shouldn't you know how a lawyer is to behave or not in your matter? These suggestions are not made for the purpose of making sure that you need to ticket the lawyer for every perceived or misperceived step out of line but rather to make you more comfortable when descending into unknown arenas of what can easily become a legal snake pit due in part to a lack of knowledge.[10]

In New Jersey the predominant publisher of Law Books of distinction is Gann Law Books whose address is One Washington Park, Suite 1500, Newark, New Jersey 07102; phone number is (973) 268-1200; and fax number is (973) 268-1330.

---

10 "Heaven helps those who help themselves."

Chapter Twenty-Six

References

Most people who need to go to a doctor to have heart surgery ask friends of other physicians as well as other sources about their selection of a surgeon. If they find out that half of the doctor's patients die on the table they are usually somewhat put off. Despite this high mortality rate early on we discussed that half of all cases are lost so the legal climb is quite uphill. You would not go to a doctor who killed half of his patients but you are stuck in the legal system to confront this type of number. A misperception is to conclude that you want a lawyer who wins eighty (80%) percent of his cases which seems logical. It does not matter if he does have such a high percentage of wins although it may be historically interesting and relevant (but not controlling) in your selection. Your case will be either won or lost and therefore the outcome of the case is a straight level of fifty-fifty. Therefore, what you really need is the lawyer willing to work on your matter until you win which then becomes one hundred percent of success.

Pre-engagement is the right time to start inquire about whether your candidate lawyer is a good speaker (or not) and if he has "the music in him." Believe me, film producers ask around about how actors are doing today because they know what they did yesterday. Are they in a love triangle relationship or addicted to drugs? Lawyers too are given to such difficulties, at least as great as the general population if not more, given the stress and pressure of the practice. Alcoholism, drug addiction, gambling just to name a few are ripe within the legal community. In the prior days particularly as to drug addicts , the lawyer with difficulties was disbarred and so the public community was not at risk to falling prey to the lawyer's problems. Now there are many good resources for lawyers who can admit their difficulties, seek treatment, and continue practicing. You are not going to get a direct answer from any lawyer realistically about how many times he has been rehabilitated for addiction. Actually what you are going to do is part company after any such question likely by being asked to leave.

It should not surprise you that most court proceedings are open to the public. Thus, a good place to search out a lawyer is in a courtroom. There you get to see him in action and his native abilities away from what you are simply being told by him or others. Many lawyers are flattered (particularly those who believe in themselves) by the request to "see them in action." They think it is part of their reputation and sale and they would love to show you their ability.

Moreover, once at the court, you get a change to ask the bailiff, the law clerk, the client of the lawyer who you may hire, and others present about whether this guy is really any good. Sheriff's officers and bailiffs are more likely to input the information than law clerks who are fresh out of law school and are most likely not to know much except what they may have heard the judge comment to them. Actually law clerks usually stay in legal chambers even during trials or proceedings. Sometimes when an important matter is about to be heard and lawyers of distinction gather about counsel table then you know something big is going on and you have probably gotten an all-star group of legal players assembled. Certainly this is a group from which to begin the search. Any court person can identify them to you.

Finally, we do not live in a closed society. We all have relatives. Lots of them work in courts and courthouses. Many of them know someone who knows a friend or relative who works in a courthouse or law firm. A word to the wise being sufficient, all you need to do is track down these people and make inquiry. Who are the best negligence lawyers; who is good at divorce matters and the like! Reputation stands for a lot in the practice of law and these people are more likely to tell you accurately. None have a forwarding fee or other agenda. They are also likely to be able to tell you if the lawyer has problems of a person nature such as alcohol or the like. Some lawyers are great up to lunch but after a drink or two cannot function in the afternoon. This is the information you want to gather up by using non-legal outside sources.

Obviously, it makes sense if you can to ask a lawyer's support staff if they think "Jack" is any good. You know already that nine times out of ten the answer is going to be positive because if it is not that employee and "Jack" have now a real problem if it gets back and they and "Jack" are not going to be friends very much longer. However, while like "Karmack, the Magician" the whole answer to the question is virtually known before the question is put in the rare instances you may be told "no" and no more time is wasted on this candidate. Indeed, the support staff members even with the predicted apparent verbal response with the wink of the eye or frown can reveal the true response despite the words of approval spoken. This placces it back to your initial instincts and interpretations "but nothing ventured is nothing gained." A lawyer is not going to be put off because you asked his support staff about him and if he is then he is not your boy. However, to get away with such a question even half heartedly (which is a good way of putting the question) you need to establish however quickly some type of rapport either when booking the appointment with the support staff as early as you can. Chit-chatting with the staff does not harm you but rather loosens up the environment.

Chapter Twenty-Seven

Avoidance Criteria

Some lawyers are simply glamorous people. Certain are overwhelmingly attractive, educated, rich, well spoken and in the category of "quite a catch". This obviously occurs in both genders. While it is nice to stand next to a pretty boy it is not the basis for engagement. If such attractiveness is being used for purposes of engagement you need to be very careful about whether the rest of this candidate's mind is otherwise untalented and empty. It should not surprise you that many of these pretty people can be found in practice areas that involve more rather than less client contact. You may actually find that those in the patent department or trademark department are less attractive but apt intellectual criteria is the order of the day in such fields.

We are all people in first blush. Obviously, it is nice to deal with a beauty queen or what your mother would consider to be first-class husband material. However, many lawyers in certain specialty departments are attractive. These people could be distracting to the jury who may become taken with them and not listen to what they say. It is what they say that matters if you are going to be helped. Also, if you find yourself socially taken to the candidate attorney then it is best not to hire them but rather to try to date them! Then you can get the benefit of their advice in the privacy of the relationship while you carry on in your case with some less attractive member of the Bar. It is not unnatural to be drawn to some people on appearances but it is not prosperous in the handling of a legal matter and is clearly to be avoided without exception.

Chapter Twenty-Eight

Confidential Understandings

In rare instances you may need a lawyer to exploit patents, trademarks or other protectable intellectual or business ideas. These can be extremely economically valuable to a lawyer who is a good method thinker but does not know anything about the exploitation of the idea or how really to protect it and therefore you. There are certain instances where you can mistakenly place your notion into the public realm and eliminate your ability to protect it. Obviously, you would not know any better until you had a lawyer's advice especially in the area of patents and other business-related ideas. Many lawyers certainly do understand these circumstances but you want to make sure there is no confusion. You are about to impart an idea or design and you do not want it exploited without your benefit. You need to avoid the lawyer who presents to you an ability to help to exploit by becoming your partner or by sending you to someone who will. There needs to be full pre-retainer disclosure with the lawyer of what they really will be. You don't want to be surprised later with a claim that because the lawyer charged a much lower or no fee that he was a financial partner of yours. Certainly what you tell the lawyer is confidential but if you think no one has even been exploited by their lawyer becoming a snake in the grass then you are incredibly naïve. Accordingly, it is preferably at the time of making the initial interview for you and your friend with the lawyer to explain that given the need to divulge to him your novel ideas you would like to have a confidentiality agreement with him and his firm so there can be no misunderstanding if for some reason (however strange) you later develop certain unresolvedable attorney-client issues and wind up some place else. Why should any well meaning person complain about the need to provide you with sufficient comfort levels of disclosure especially when the nature of things are that confidentiality agreements are the common order of the day in such matters? It is no skin off the lawyer's back and it shows a predisposition to understand your needs and to otherwise "do the right thing."

Chapter Twenty-Nine

Safekeeping of Funds

In some disputes it will be necessary to discuss the deposit of money at the outset with an attorney you are about to engage. This may be true in real estate or other matters. Routinely deposits of ten percent more or less in a real estate transaction can be deposited with the lawyer, the title company, broker. Naturally, it depends on the size of the transaction. If you buy a shopping mall for $30 million then a $3 million deposit is significant.

In making these types of transactions with a lawyer the best thing to understand is that you do not know (and cannot) about the integrity of the law firm's staff and who already stole what money from the trust account. By the time you get any missing funds back (if you do at all) the value of it will have declined and it will have still been unavailable to you when you needed it. If large sums are to be involved, you need to reach an understanding a the beginning that you want them deposited in a public facility that is FDIC insured or in reliable top level investments such as treasury notes and treasury bills that avoid the risk of loss since the loss can be greater than the funds. For example, if you promised to buy the shopping mall and your deposit has been stolen you still need to come up with it again to close your purchase. If you cannot, you still might get sued for the entire purchase amount due at closing particularly if it was a $30 million purchase which is now valued at $20 million because of changes in the economy. If you consider that this problem was created by the theft and the delay in trying to get back these funds then you have put yourself at a terrible risk by not seeing to your own best needs at the outset in the attorney-client relationship. No lawyer should care where you want the funds deposited as long as there is an understanding of integrity in the institution and they are not being put in specious South African gold-mining stocks.

Chapter Thirty

Certain Concerns

When you are hiring a lawyer at an hourly rate, you will very often find that what you are being told of the hourly-rate terms in the beginning, may be adjusted upward. No one ever heard of lawyers lowering voluntarily their hourly rates over prior years (except as negotiated from time to time artfully by a client and/or their consultant). It should be your intention to determine what is the rate and the real understanding that your matter will be seen through to a conclusion without any upward advancement by the lawyer and his staff.[11]

Many lawyers' retainers will include reference to fixed fee services. This is not objectionable but some lawyers have a published fee schedule for them and some do not. The fixed

---

11 Many law firms change hourly rates for subordinate staff members which also increase.

fees are generated by an intention to keep down the necessity of overall fee expenses. When done properly they are a good attempt to minimize fees rather than to churn the file and enhance them. What it means is if your lawyer charges $400.00 per hour but needs to put together a subpoena for a time, date and place and pulls the file to do so and studies the documents you might end up spending one-half hour in time for a $200.00 service than enjoying a fixed fee for half that sum.

The retainer agreement will also indicate billing time periods. Old versus young lawyers have actual billing time periods based on how their practice evolved. It is not uncommon for billing periods to be a minimum of one-quarter hour or one-tenth of an hour. The difficulty is that it remains a matter of money and billing. The result may yet be the same. You are billed for fifteen minutes of time or six minutes (the lowest billing period) of time regardless of whether the time took two or three minutes. Invariably the time is rounded up to the fullest billing period but the retainer should so indicate so everyone knows how it works and not telling you is worse than faithfully disclosing at the outset such matters. There is no error of billing by the lawyer and there are different reasons for it. One is no better than the other. Lawyers are not time clocks and holding them to such confines and standards may not always be a good idea.

This is true because such higher billing-period lawyers are not setting about to over bill you (having set forth how it works) but because it is an intellectual undertaking. Now if you think that they are only intending to sit around and bill you respectively for every one-tenth of an hour for the providing routine work, calls, and advice (which still is perfectly natural) you should anticipate that there should be many discussions to develop your matter. An experienced lawyer does not just make a telephone call. He thinks about your case; he thinks about what your needs are; and then he sets about it. Although the telephone itself may be less limited in time to the total undertaking, you should be concentrating on his thought process rather than the time clock punching and it is up to the lawyer to tell you what billing he prefers as to his rates and to what he thinks he is entitled.[12] He is entitled to set his own fee standard especially if you found the lawyer you want while you may still to do your best in getting a reduced rate. It is a mutual undertaking and can be guided only by mutually acceptable circumstances. He knows what you want and is ready, willing and able to actually try to deliver to you. So you need to accept what he is telling you (assuming it is sensible and true) and you either get together professionally or you do not.

---

12 Also, a too sharpened pencil can stab you. If the project takes two or three hours than the final billing period is miniscule by comparison.

A real lawyer will tell you the way it is or the way it isn't because he knows what input from you that he is going to require and of the ultimate need for it. He may simply feel that he cannot (or will not) do "sophisticated surgery with stone age tools." A real lawyer is not going to blame you for trying to cut his fees back but sometimes you too have to wise up because you are on the legal playing field.[13] You sometimes have to "close your eyes and pay full price." You may be confused (without help) but this does not necessarily mean that you can alter the lawyer's billing practices rather than the rate itself. Obviously, it can become a big concern. One-quarter hour at $400.00 per hour is $100.00 and the same one-quarter hour at $300.00 per hour is $75.00. This is where the savings occurs and not in telling the lawyer about established billing periods and how he should alter with them for you.

In addressing these circumstances some people clearly make a mistake of bending over in the wrong direction. They become too cavalier about the projected expenses as though money did not mean anything to them. This is not a good idea. Sooner or later in the law (principles aside) it all boils down to money.

Away from being cavalier, you should also avoid in any initial interview signs of affluence. Take off your Rolex, diamonds, and

---

13 Note bene: The game is not controlled by the billing period but by the rate.

pearls and leave the Bentley Concourse at home and take the Subaru. Who knows who is going to spot you in the parking lot? You are not there to impress anyone by being draped in gold with the projection of wealth (or what you project it to be). Any such display is certainly going to make any lawyer want to help you to get their share of the golden egg. If you can sport an expensive handbag you can be sure the lawyer knows what it is because he has most likely paid for plenty of them at home. Even the most unassuming lawyer understands the scent of money. Now if you live in a rich community it is a little difficult not to tell your lawyer candidate that you are from Beverly Hills. It is also unnecessary to place yourself in a circumstance where you are obviously going to be the focus of an attempt to open your wallet. However obvious, this is nothing more than common sense.[14] Likewise, it would be ridiculous for you to appear to be a pauper and for your friend to appear to be as prosperous as a well-paid movie actor while you live next door to each other in the same rich town. Dress down! For example, in a matter where you are being sued for punitive damages that does not mean you have to reveal at the beginning interview when you are forming your relationship that you have vast assets.

---

14 Let's say instinct.

Chapter Thirty-One

Avoiding Your Own Mistakes

Assume now that you spent time, effort and money in locating perhaps even up to one-half dozen choices for your lawyer. You have done everything you can to develop you relationship also with the support staff. You have established a comfort level in your matter and the point is not to waste it needlessly. Lawyers like light switches can be turned "on" and turned "off" by people and their appearances. Some people think their own type-A dominant influence ability is disproportionately in their favor. In speaking to a lawyer and sitting and hearing their advice and willingness to help, some people get literally carried away. They slit their own throat of any realistic relationship at the beginning. Most of the ways of doing so are not innocent but upon reflection just simply unclever if you are setting out to get someone to help you out. You also need to project to the lawyer that you are "okay" and socially acceptable ad a great person too. To sit there and explain to the lawyer that you have a friend who is a judge who you spoke to already and who knows the court people involved and will help behind the scenes to make a good result happen. Now you ask you candidate what can he do to help this along which reflects your total lack of belief in the justice system itself and your own predisposition to work around it. Alternatively maybe you inquire if a better result can be had if your intention is to present what you should both know to be inappropriate evidence. Likewise there may yet be other topics of "discussion" (sic: misdiscussion) or what an easily prompt other matters of legitimate concern to the lawyer about you. These are ideas or "helpful" suggestion that will be rejected out of hand by any well-meaning lawyer although you may find the lawyer still willing to take your case. Why? The reason is simple. Once you have exposed yourself as a potential lowlife then the lawyer may simply memo his own file that you made these inappropriate suggestions and when push comes to shove in your relationship you may well be confronted with your own errant behavior to make you go away. Accordingly, you have taken what could have been a good professional contact and lost or sullied it. Likewise in terms of dealing with lawyers there may be many things he does not need to know and you do not help yourself by revealing what could be a history of your own negative behavior.

Naturally, if you hire the lawyer for a divorce matter or for a slip and fall it is not required that you volunteer that you routinely commit adultery or have a girlfriend. While this may be of greater important in the divorce sphere, it is only relevant if such accusations are placed. You cannot obtain a divorce form your girlfriend and whether he suspects you have one or not (however interesting) may not be particularly relevant. Now, however, the lawyer knows about it because you bragged needlessly or actually brought her with you he is playing for two: one of which (the girlfriend) does not really care what he has paid as long as the divorce occurs. This is particularly more true if your assets are substantial. You have exposed your own bones for picking.

Again consider that you are going to sell your small convenience store that you have had for years. How and under what circumstances you are going to do so should be your business. Now when you go to the lawyer and tell him that the deal is for one-half million dollars but you want a contract for $300,000.00 because you are going to get $200,000.00 in cash at the closing you are asking him to participate in fraud and a knowing crime. What you can expect later on and how much are you really going to pay such a lawyer for helping to launder money?

Similarly to tell them that you annually take another $150,000.00 in cash out of the business is quite unnecessary. Everybody knows that this occurs to some degree. However, it is unclever for you to so volunteer and then try to embroil the lawyer in your history of errant behavior which need remain private. Now considering realistically that it is no longer a routine interview because of your disclosures to the lawyer it now becomes one of great value where you want him to stray over the line of scrimmage to try and insulate you in a dishonorable transaction. What could have been a closing for a few thousand dollars is going to cost you a lot more in the long run in fees and likely exposure should you argue with such a lawyer in the future. In such disputes a layer may no longer be bound by a confidential attorney-client privilege and may divulge your own blackheartedness (dishonesty) in his favor in your dispute. The likelihood of you being shaken down by your own deeds and bras someday later on exists. If push comes to shove the lawyer may disclose the paperwork you gave him showing how for example what it was in paperwork that you used to convince the buyer that the books themselves were not the real reflection of the business value and earnings.

When you reveal to a lawyer something that was clearly unnecessary to your matter you may expect it to be disclosed later on. Lawyers know at the beginning how to best protect themselves against you in the future because that is a common experience and most lawyers have an old rolodex of former best friends. A better conclusion would be to not fail to appreciate an understanding of this message. Lawyers are at least as fit as you are in knowing how to deal with you in future adversity than are you. They are more experience at it; better suited; and have been down many more rough roads than you have. If you think that you are going to best him (because somehow in your perception you thrive on it) then you might as well tell the doctor you intend to stay up during the surgical procedure. You can predict the likelihood of your own nonsuccess easily in both situations.

Chapter Thirty-Two

Preparation

Statistically well more than nine out of ten cases settle. So what! It is unimportant to predict if yours will. The chances of predicting if this may occur is of no value because it lulls you into a false security not to prepare your case. Obviously, although frequently a positive settlement outcome is had there can be no counting on it. Accordingly, that means that you have to plan at the very beginning with your candidate lawyer that your case needs to be prepared fully for trial at all stages of the proceeding. Doing so in a manner the adversary will understand so as for him to become motivated to settle with you. Also of initial concern is that sometimes you give a lawyer great evidence. Some lawyer's concept is to play a cat and mouse game with it so that they attempt to hold it back and use it in a surprise manner much later on or only at trial. This is not what a client wants. Very often what happens is that the evidence is excluded and you are sitting there on your hands without a great case any longer. Accordingly remitting full and complete discovery needs to be agreed upon at the outset especially when you have the winning evidence. Revealing it early on may also help to provoke an early settlement and save you legal fees if you have followed how to make better arrangements effectively as earlier set forth.

Discovery is about revealing what exists. It includes depositions, interrogatories and disclosure of evidence and proofs which must be done well in advance of what is considered the discovery end (cut-off) date which is initially set forth in the court's pretrial schedule when the matter is filed at the time the suit has begun. This means that you have to show your cards in full. Accordingly, at the initial interview you should mention at least your casual knowledge that there will be such discovery and the fact that you want all of your proofs and evidence put forward and timely disclosed. You should further explain that well before your deposition (several weeks) and well before the trial (several weeks again) you need to be prepared and reprepared for your testimony particularly in case you have any questions that arise. Many lawyers will simply agree upon this full style of preparation at the beginning but instead call you in the morning of your deposition and chat with you for a few minutes and leave you to your own devices including saying something negative as to your case. Should this occur you need to tell the lawyer to reschedule a deposition and find out why the preparation protocols failed and rethinking if you are still at the right place. Most usually you know well in advance the trial date or should, but even then some lawyers will call you the night before. Again this needs to be sorted out in you favor or you case remain jeopardized. Bring your interview friend and diary to confirm it was agreed at the outset interview that this was not to have happened. It should not have occurred if you were calling the lawyer and support staff regularly. It likely also would not have occurred if you had used a consultant and had them follow up on you matter. You might now indeed need to tell the court you went to a new lawyer. Good luck.

Likewise, most lawyers will simply send you the interrogatories to be answered which is not objectionable in first blush. What you really need to know to discuss at the beginning is that you request to know that your candidate lawyer will sit with you and help answer them so that you are fully responsive and made your disclosure. It is not wise if you are unprepared and it is certainly not the best course for your matter. With such initial discussion had, it may disclose that the lawyer's office practices may well not suit your case needs. Some lawyers may take a casual approach to the working up of the matter because they are focusing elsewhere on the trial or on settlement, but this is not where you need or want to be. Showing that you understand with routine knowledge certain aspects of discovery certainly does not make you look bad at the beginning interview but rather suggests that you are a better-informed legal player. It is contrary to a positive outcome to pass yourself off initially as uninformed or unclever. How could anyone consider this to be so if you come with a shopping list of sensible requirements so everybody to be involved is very clear how your matter is going to proceed.

Chapter Thirty-Three

Appeals

Your trial is over and you know in which fifty percent category you have landed. You lost! Too bad for you! Now how are you going to get out of the snake pit alive? If you become convicted of a crime you have every right to have a specialty sentencing lawyer to speak for you now including any hearings about sentence which occur in serious matters such as death penalty hearings. There are lawyers who are experienced in defending those to be sentenced post conviction, and just because you are convicted doesn't mean that you should not have one. Why continue with someone with a negative outcome? Let the jury understand there are new player lawyers for a new player group on your behalf that they might relate to better. Think about it. As a client you do not want to get sentenced. Your lawyer is not a sentencing expert. Also, a sentencing lawyer might be attuned to why you were convicted in the first place, perhaps due to ineffective assistance of counsel issues. It is a second set of eyes and helping hands used to minimize any sentence before you have crossed over by receiving it.

You cannot really expect your losing trial lawyer to best fully appreciate appeal, the failing decision, or outcome. It requires a calm fresh look and evaluation. Even if he did, the likelihood of his exposing himself to self criticism of his own trial handling (sic: mishandling) of you matter does not help you very much and your sentencing or new lawyer might bring curative motions yet now might serve to help you with the trial outcome or create further relief issues preserved on appeal.

Appeals are a specialty practice that require substantial experienced over the years in bringing them. Appellate Judges are different than trial judges and march to a different tune in their standard of review and the art of persuasion required at the trial level is hardly the same at the Appellate level. Nevertheless, appellate lawyers really develop from a steeped history in trial practice and to become a good appellate lawyer you need to be enhanced with a substantial history of trial background including specifically in the area of law to be appealed. How can one as an appeal lawyer spot and reveal difficulties occurring historically at the trial level without any real background understanding where the errors in a specialized legal area were made earlier at trial? If you never tried a case in the legal area involved then why would you be able to take an effective appeal in a sophisticated legal matter? Accordingly you will find that most established appellate lawyers are not simply to be found in the appellate Section of some big firm doing nothing else with no trial experience but rather "practice trials and appeals" and are so listed in most directories. Thus, it is necessary to inquire whether your Appeal requires an experienced Appeals attorney. Appellate Judges come from the same areas at the trial levels are well known and usually relate to those individuals who routinely appear in front of them and are considered to be with the Appellate Bar.

Interestingly enough the most glaring exception to the rule is the United States Supreme Court. Recently Justice Sonia Sotomayor was appointed, and just prior to which Justice Samuel Alito was appointed to the Court. Both appointments were supported by the fact that these two new Justices alone were a breath of fresh air because they enjoyed some history of trial experience making their thoughts able to include an intellectual trial background.

If you have the need to appeal the essential criteria for it is to get at once a new set of eyes. How can you really expect the trial lawyer to understand how things went wrong in your law ship while he was at the helm? Even if he did so there is a high likelihood that he may now not have revealed it because it would become a point of criticism; malpractice; or ultimate dispute about fees. In many states a lawyer who has malpracticed you is not entitled to a fee and is required to return whatever fees they obtained from the outset. Obviously then, legal points that need to be raised upon appeal cannot rely upon the same set of trial eyes. This might even lead to an uninsured event under any legal malpractice policy if a trial lawyer revealed for appeal his own error which might betoken the defense carrier a lack of cooperation in the conditions of the legal malpractice policy. This realistically is not going to happen and so you need a new set of eyes. Obviously, this excludes the old law firm of the lawyer himself. Do you think someone in the appellate section of his law firm is going to reveal what we just discussed and that no lawyer would do to himself? You lost your case and the time has come to move on to new players for your benefit. This is one of the primary reasons why there are specialty lawyers handling sentencing and appellate matters. Regardless to say you are back to your search to find who can help save the day at this late date. Obviously, as a final caution if you can not deal with your trial lawyer and you can not deal with his law firm you need to totally avoid any referral from them about where else to go. If you avoid this advice, you can be certain only that you will be most likely directed to someone with whom there is a friendship of a significant level to bar him from further revealing the trial sins of the past of your foremen referring lawyers who also might receive fees sent back to them all for the result of losing you case due to their oversight.

Chapter Thirty-Four

How to Replace Your Lawyer

Now that you have read this book, suppose that you have already fallen into a legal honey trap, you need to realistically consider how and when to replace your lawyer. What are your full choices? The first thing of course is to stand pat; take no cards and move forth down the road of your mistake. Not a very practical solution! The other best course is to decide to move on to greener pastures.

However unsettling, this is not uncommon but you can now continue with the benefit of this book to guide you out of hot water. Probably 20% or more matters are the subject of replacement counsel well before their completion. You should change lawyers as you change doctors when you see the need. However, long before you die on the operating table of life (those of doctors and lawyers) you need to continue along with a professional who can realistically help you move forward. While these problems appear to be fully negative there is also a potential for a renaissance effect on your case. It is a "stop, look, and listen" wake-up call to the adversarial lawyer on the other side. They are drawn to realize that knowing now where the matter ends with your current lawyer and with your case that you have decided to beef it up by moving on to better counsel. Likewise, a new consulting-reviewing attorney or a chosen replacement can tell you to what degree your case has been jeopardized; how best to reconstruct it if possible; and whether you have been malpracticed. Remember the earlier statement in prior Chapters that in most states a lawyer who has mishandled your matter can not collect his balance (fee) due and would likely have to disgorge the monies already received. If your matter is contingent, you can oppose their participation fee based on negligent prior behavior since the second replacement lawyer likely knows of the first lawyers professional errors and that he now is to recover the first lawyer's to a case in progress. The contingent fee not going to the first lawyer should be yours to keep but you may owe the second lawyer some fee for collecting that now unless this were something that you and your consultant covered effectively at the time of the second engagement.

Epilogue

This is not a work of fiction but rather a work of personal belief developed over the experience of more than four decades including as the son of a lawyer. These are matters of the author's perception. Could the author be in error about such conclusions? Certainly but I do not think I am.

This is a how-to help yourself publication. It tries best to emphasize what foundation information you should consider (or reject) as you alone see fit. The book is not and is not intended to be legal advice. It is to be used as a guide only to help you sort out the basis for decisions you may wish to make in the conduct affecting your own legal affairs. Neither is it about any criticism of the legal system but rather an attempt to set forth a floor plan of how it works as you elect to enter it. It is for you and you alone to accept or reject the ideas put forth as you see fit. Good luck.

Appendix

About the Author, Curriculum Vitae of Author

Consulting Agreement is available with the Author to utilize it to locate a selection of attorneys and to lower attorney's fees with a potential return of the consulting fees paid upon a successful outcome. This particularly applies to legal-medical malpractice matters and general negligence, tort matters, workmen's compensation and commercial-business litigation.

About the Author

STEPHEN SCHNITZER, ESQ.

PRESIDENT: STEPHEN SCHNITZER, ESQ., P.A.

A Professional Corporation

40 West Northfield Road

P.O. Box 691

Livingston, New Jersey 07039-0691

(973) 533-1212 Tel.

(973) 533-0502 Fax.

CURRICULUM VITAE OF AUTHOR

Stephen Schnitzer, born Newark, New Jersey, April 6, 1943; admitted to New Jersey bar, 1968, New Jersey; 1972, U.S. Supreme Court. Preparatory education, The Johns Hopkins University (B.A., 1965); legal education, Rutgers University (J.D., 1968). Member, Rutgers Law Review, 1966-1967, 1967-1968. Law Lecturer, Suffolk Law School, 1968-1969. Special Assistant to Administrative Director of the Court, Honorable Edward O'Connel, 1965. Law Secretary to Honorable Sidney Goldmann, Presiding Judge, Appellate Division, 1968-1969; New Jersey Supreme Court, pro tem. Assistant Essex County Prosecutor, 1970. General Counsel, New Jersey Quarter Horse Association, Inc., 1975 and forward; G.J. Chemical Co., Inc. and associated entities, 1985-; Krajack Tank Lines, Inc., 1985-; Vitusa Products, Inc. and its affiliate chemical distribution entities, 1986-. Member, Advisory Board, Organization of Women for Legal Awareness, 1976-. Member: Essex County, New Jersey State, Federal (Member, Counsel on Antitrust and Trade Regulation, 1974-) and American (Charter Member, 1973- and Member, Circuit Committee of the Business Torts subsection, Section on Litigation, 1974-, Member, Sections on: Antitrust Law; Family Law; Criminal Justice. Bar Associations; The Association of Trial Lawyers of America; American Judicature Society. Appointed United States Federal Court arbitrator (1987) District of New Jersey; member of HALT, the organization of Americans for Legal Reform: listed for years last past in the directory of Legal Malpractice Attorneys 1989 to date. Qualified and engaged as a legal malpractice expert statewide in the areas including but not limited to Civil Procedure, Real Estate, Real Estate Titles, Criminal law, Matrimonial law, general and complex litigation, bankruptcy, foreclosure, general practice and related matters. Author: The Pitfalls of How, When, Where and Why to Hire Lawyers; Bad Vespers, "A Novel of Assassination"; Adam & Eve & Rick & Jane By God a 12/21/2012 Revelation.

Consulting Agreement

The author operates a consulting entity for purposes of implementing the concept proffered in book. It is a consulting service and not legal advice. The consulting arrangement can be discussed by contacting the author directly as follows:

STEPHEN SCHNITZER, ESQ.

PRESIDENT: STEPHEN SCHNITZER, ESQ., P.A.

A Professional Corporation

40 West Northfield Road

P.O. Box 691

Livingston, New Jersey 07039-0691

(973) 533-0622 Tel.

(973)533-0502 Fax.

E-mail: maldemer12@verizon.net

The author proffers to attempt to recommend qualified counsel in accordance with the protocols set forth in the book and to estimate a negotiation of the lowering of the traditional attorney's fees charge by the various law firms to be considered. In aid thereof, the author proposes within the consulting arrangement to participate in the reduction of fees and to return the consulting fee paid on the successful outcome of the legal matter involved to the degree that the fee arrangement results in a payment equal to or greater than the consulting fee. If a lesser amount is received then it will be returned. The object is to use the consulting opportunity with the expectation that it may lead to a positive outcome including the reduction of legal fees and in many cases the return of the consulting fees paid to accomplish a positive outcome.

Bibliography & Suggested Reading

"Listen to Leaders In the Law"

"The New Jersey Court Rules to Date"

"The Bramble Bush" by Karl Llewellyn

"Martindale-Hubbell"

"Gann Law Books"

Alice in Wonderland – looking down the looking glass